THE VICTORIAN AND EDWARDIAN TOURIST

John Hannavy

Published in Great Britain in 2012 by Shire Publications Ltd, Midland House, West Way, Botley, Oxford OX2 0PH, United Kingdom.

44-02 23rd Street, Suite 219, Long Island City, NY 11101, USA.

E-mail: shire@shirebooks.co.uk   www.shirebooks.co.uk

© 2012 John Hannavy.

All rights reserved. Apart from any fair dealing for the purpose of private study, research, criticism or review, as permitted under the Copyright, Designs and Patents Act, 1988, no part of this publication may be reproduced, stored in a retrieval system, or transmitted in any form or by any means, electronic, electrical, chemical, mechanical, optical, photocopying, recording or otherwise, without the prior written permission of the copyright owner. Enquiries should be addressed to the Publishers.

Every attempt has been made by the Publishers to secure the appropriate permissions for materials reproduced in this book. If there has been any oversight we will be happy to rectify the situation and a written submission should be made to the Publishers.

A CIP catalogue record for this book is available from the British Library.

Shire Library no. 692.   ISBN-13: 978 0 74781 153 4

John Hannavy has asserted his right under the Copyright, Designs and Patents Act, 1988, to be identified as the author of this book.

Designed by Tony Truscott Designs, Sussex, UK and typeset in Perpetua and Gill Sans.

Printed in China through Worldprint Ltd.

12 13 14 15 16   10 9 8 7 6 5 4 3 2 1

COVER IMAGE
A group of American tourists poses for the camera in front of the building on Portsmouth Street, London, described by Charles Dickens as the location of the Old Curiosity Shop; from a postcard published *c.* 1908.

TITLE PAGE IMAGE
A paddle-steamer carries tourists to inspect the final few weeks of work on the construction of the Forth Bridge. This lantern slide was taken in 1889, and behind the steamer can be seen the hull of one of the supply ships which ferried construction materials out to the bridge. Tourist sailings under the bridge remained popular for many years after it opened – especially if the rumble of a steam train overhead could be heard.

CONTENTS PAGE IMAGE
This tinted postcard shows an ancient street in Lacock, Wiltshire, and was published in 1903. For small villages, where sales were likely to be slow, it would have been uneconomic for the postcard companies to commission new photography, so they often reused old pictures. The original photograph used for the postcard was taken more than thirty years earlier, in the late 1860s or very early 1870s. The man on the right is Joseph Foden, the village carpenter who made the wooden bodies of some of the first cameras ever built. His crude and simple little box cameras were used in the 1830s by William Henry Fox Talbot, squire of Lacock Abbey, and the man who invented the photographic negative and set the world along the road which made tourist photography possible. One of the original card-mounted cabinet-size prints – a little over twice the size of a carte-de-visite – survives in the Foden family.

ACKNOWLEDGEMENTS
All illustrations are from the author's collection except the following, which are acknowledged with thanks:

Ashbee Archive, 13, 94 (bottom), 116; Christie's 33 (top); Rob Neiderman, 119 (middle); Thomas Cook Archive 18 (inset), 24, 26 (top left and right), 27, 28 (inset), 29 (inset), 31 (top), 32, 34–6, 37 (top and bottom right), 51 (bottom), 83 (top), 104 (insets), 106, 107 (inset).

Shire Publications is supporting the Woodland Trust, the UK's leading woodland conservation charity, by funding the dedication of trees.

CONTENTS

PREFACE	4
TRAVELLING IN TIME	6
THOMAS COOK'S TOURS	24
THE UBIQUITOUS GUIDEBOOK	38
DAVID MACBRAYNE'S ROYAL ROUTES	52
EXPLORING THE ENGLISH LAKES	64
'ON THE CONTINONG'	76
MEMENTOES OF AN ITALIAN TOUR	88
TAKING THE GRAND TOUR OF EGYPT	104
TOURING WITH A CAMERA	116
INDEX	128

Top: A party of ladies about to embark on a tour of New York in 1905/6 on board an electric-powered charabanc. Going on a tour was a significant social statement, and tourists wanted to be seen in their best clothes.

Middle: A group of American tourists dressed in the latest fashions poses outside the Old Curiosity Shop made famous by Charles Dickens.

Right: A Blackpool circular tour tram laden with visitors pauses for the postcard photographer's camera *c.* 1910.

PREFACE

A S SOMEONE who has toured the world extensively with my own camera over the years – most notably for my book *Great Photographic Journeys – In the Footsteps of Pioneer British Photographers* (Dewi Lewis, 2007), exploring how our predecessors did it has held an enduring fascination for me.

Unpicking the story of the evolution of the travel industry during the Victorian and Edwardian years has been rewarding, and gathering together a representative collection of images and artefacts which define that evolution has been a fascinating challenge. I am grateful to the many people who have answered my questions on the subject.

My thanks go to John and Kathryn Carruthers, Michael Gray, Roger Taylor, everyone who has pointed me towards engaging contemporary accounts of Victorian and Edwardian tourism, and especially to Paul Smith and the Thomas Cook Group plc for assistance with the costings of Victorian and Edwardian travel, the development of package tours, and for the use of so much original material from the Thomas Cook Archive.

I have drawn heavily from Baedeker's *Guides*, Thomas Cook's many publications, and the little books produced by Ward, Locke & Co and A. & C. Black, as well as the many other Victorian publishers whose guidebooks not only helped their contemporaries appreciate and understand their tourist experiences, but also provide us today with fascinating insights into the lives of our Victorian and Edwardian predecessors.

Very special thanks, as always, to my wife Kath for her constant support and encouragement.

John Hannavy, Great Cheverell, 2012

Two men with their ox-sleigh prepare to take a touring couple for an excursion; Madeira, c. 1905.

TRAVELLING IN TIME

Even in the early years of the nineteenth century, the word 'tourist' had rarely, if ever, been heard. The young men, and the wealthy families, who in the eighteenth century travelled across Europe in search of experience and cultural enrichment would not have described themselves as 'tourists'. They might have done the 'Grand Tour', but they would have identified themselves as wealthy travellers, or 'voyagers'.

It is unclear exactly when the word 'tour' assumed its modern meaning, and when the terms 'tourist' and 'tourism' were first used. Uses of 'tour' to describe a circular journey – ending up back where one started – can be traced back as far as the mid-seventeenth century. 'Tourism' and 'tourist', however, probably did not appear until a century and a half later – 'tourist' around 1800, and 'tourism' a decade or so afterwards.

By the time Queen Victoria came to the throne in 1837, there were already instances of the word 'tourist' being used almost as a pejorative term by the wealthy elite, but at the same time tourism was being seen as an opportunity for enlightenment, excitement and experience by the middle classes, whose social status such tours might enhance.

At first, once the words had drifted into common usage, the term 'tourist' was generally used to describe someone who travelled abroad on holiday. Thus British tourists were those who visited Europe or went further afield, while in France tourists were primarily those who crossed the Channel to visit Britain.

Opposite: Tourists gather in front of the fifteenth-century Zytglogge Tower in Bern, Switzerland, just before midday to watch the larger than life-size gilded figure of a burgher striking the great bell.

Below: London Victoria station in 1902, still displaying the name of the London, Chatham & Dover Railway, and offering 'the shortest steam mail route to France'.

7

THE VICTORIAN AND EDWARDIAN TOURIST

A 'Somali village' at the Bradford Exhibition of 1904. 2.5 million people attended the exhibition, which was intended as a celebration of the opening of the city's Cartwright Hall, but had evolved into a World Fair. Seeing how other cultures lived inevitably increased interest in travel.

A picnic at the Dropping Stone, Gilsland, Northumberland, 1860s. Charabanc outings to the countryside became annual excursions for city-based clubs and groups.

TRAVELLING IN TIME

By the 1840s, however, that distinction had been lost, and a 'Tourist' – surprisingly frequently printed with a capital 'T' – had come to mean anyone travelling away from home for leisure and pleasure. In *Sylvan's Pictorial Handbook to the English Lakes*, published in 1847, the Tourist is afforded the same formality of title as Professor, Bishop or General.

With the growth of tourism came the need for information about the places to be visited. 'The increasing demand for illustrated guide books to aid the tourist in his rambles,' wrote Sylvan (with a lower-case 't' this time), 'together with the increased facilities of railway communication, has suggested a want which the present work is intended to supply,' adding that 'it is not too much to assert that the number of Tourists will annually increase.'

Other writers followed. Charles Roger's delightful 1851 book *A Week at Bridge of Allan* offered the same justification:

Above: Welsh farmer's daughter: a tinted carte-de-visite, 1860s, by the London Stereoscopic & Photographic Company.

Middle: Bolton Castle, North Yorkshire: a tinted stereo view, 1854, by the eminent Victorian photographer Roger Fenton.

Left: Melrose Abbey, also by Fenton, 1854. Fenton employed staff at his photographic printing works in London to meet the high demand for his stereoscopic views.

9

THE VICTORIAN AND EDWARDIAN TOURIST

Ritual bathing at one of the many stepped ghats (cremation sites) on the banks of the Ganges at Benares (now Varanasi) in India. Organised trips to India, arranged by companies such as Cox & Kings, had been possible for decades before this 1908 postcard was published. There were thousands of British residents in India, in government and commerce, so organised excursions for visiting family members were commonplace.

A work portable and suitable, descriptive of scenes at and around Bridge of Allan, remarkable for their historical or natural beauty, having long been desiderated by Tourists and Visiters [sic] alike, the Author of this Volume has attempted to supply the deficiency.

Such books suffered from one deficiency which it was beyond the ability of publishers to rectify: the inclusion of photographs in books would not become practicable for some years. When it did become possible around 1850, it was initially through the expensive and labour-intensive practice of pasting actual photographic prints onto the pages. The task of pasting the pictures into the books was undertaken by teams of low-paid part-time women workers, but, with production costs significantly greater, the selling price of photographically illustrated guidebooks was much higher than that of those with conventional engravings.

The mid-1840s were crucial years in the development of tourism. Visitors had been touring the country for centuries before then, albeit in small numbers, but events in the middle of that decade established tourist traditions and expectations which endure to this day.

William Henry Fox Talbot, who had recently invented the calotype process of early photography, had the highly original idea of using photography to create an illustrated travelogue. Previously, all such books had either been unillustrated, or illustrated with engravings and woodcuts.

TRAVELLING IN TIME

For those unable to visit the exotic east, countries such as Japan could be brought to London. International exhibitions celebrated the culture and industry of far-off places, and brought visitors in their millions. These postcards, published by James Valentine, show how lavishly constructed Edwardian exhibitions were. The top postcard shows an enactment of the 'Feast of the Bear'. To the left are two views of the 'Uji Village', which was constructed on the White City site for the Japanese-British Exhibition in 1910. Such exhibitions had a considerable impact in raising interest in travel and tourism.

11

SUN PICTURES IN SCOTLAND.

Preparing for publication in 1 vol. royal 4to.

TWENTY-THREE PHOTOGRAPHIC VIEWS

IN

SCOTLAND,

BY

H. FOX TALBOT, Esq.

Price to Subscribers, One Guinea.

Subscribers names will be received by J. Rodwell, Bookseller, New Bond Street, London.

Most of the views represent scenes connected with the life and writings of Sir Walter Scott. Among them will be found—

ABBOTSFORD, | LOCH KATRINE,
MELROSE ABBEY, | DRYBURGH ABBEY,
DOUNE CASTLE, | HERIOT'S HOSPITAL,
SIR W. SCOTT'S MONUMENT, EDINBURGH.

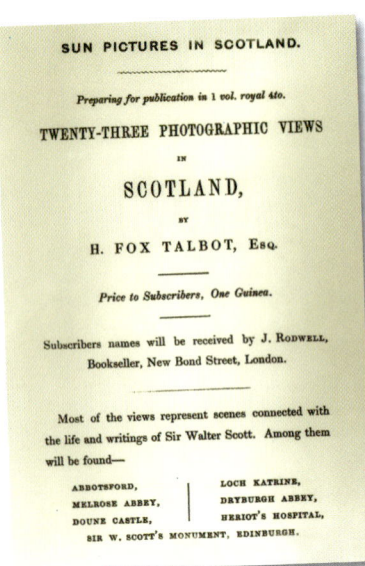

In the autumn of 1845 Talbot travelled from Wiltshire to Scotland in order to create a photographic portfolio inspired by the life and work of Sir Walter Scott, who had died less than twenty years earlier – and whose house, and the areas about which he had written, were already drawing increasing numbers of visitors.

The success of Scott's novels and epic poems had been widespread, and endures to this day. At his mock-baronial home at Abbotsford near Melrose in the Scottish Borders, he had written some of the most popular books of the time, weaving into the narrative evocative descriptions of Scotland's rugged scenery and beautiful lochs. Queen Victoria's love of Scotland had further enhanced the country's appeal. Talbot's idea was simple – to use his primitive camera to capture authentic views of the places about which Scott had written.

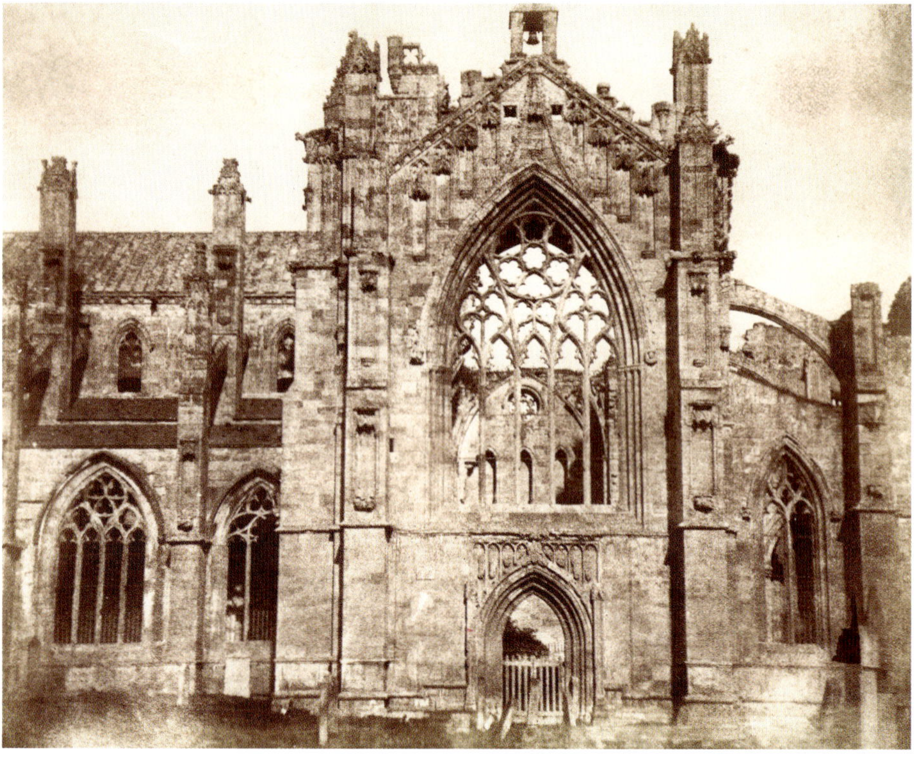

The camera was still a novelty at the time, and the perceived wonder of photography was its ability to capture the most minute detail in all its glory – detail which was invariably discarded by the painter and engraver. Thus, Talbot's photographs would reveal Sir Walter Scott's Scotland as it had never before been seen, except by those who had visited the country themselves. The resulting portfolio of twenty-three photographs was published in 1846 under the title *Sun Pictures in Scotland*, and individual prints from the series were later sold in their hundreds. Scott's tomb at Dryburgh Abbey and the partially completed Scott Monument on Princes Street, Edinburgh, were among the most popular. *Sun Pictures in Scotland* was the first publication to tap into the tourist market. Talbot had revealed a potential goldmine for the new medium.

In the same year, Thomas Cook, the organiser of a temperance group in Leicestershire, having already arranged day trips to temperance rallies, attempted something on a grander scale. He organised a tour of Scotland, for a price of one guinea covering train and steamer transport, but excluding food or accommodation – in temperance hotels, naturally. Three hundred and fifty people signed up for that trip.

Cook's travellers journeyed from Leicester to Fleetwood on chartered Midland Railway trains. There they boarded an overnight steamer which ferried them to Ardrossan on the Clyde coast – the cross-border railway line did not open until 1850 – where they were met by another chartered train. Their journey took them to Edinburgh, Stirling, Glasgow, Loch Lomond and Loch Long. The package tour to Scotland had been born.

When the cross-border railway routes opened, shipping companies lost a great deal of their passenger traffic, but most of them fought back vigorously. For the independent traveller, there were already regular paddle-steamer services from London to Edinburgh, Perth and Aberdeen, and from Liverpool to Glasgow, and all of them, by the middle of the 1850s, were offering attractive tourist fares.

But Cook had revolutionised the market. Whereas the wealthier echelons of society had already become quite used to

Opposite:
A study of Melrose Abbey in the Scottish Borders by William Henry Fox Talbot, from the portfolio *Sun Pictures in Scotland*, published in 1846.

Building the Scott Monument, Princes Street, Edinburgh, by William Henry Fox Talbot, from *Sun Pictures in Scotland*, 1846.

THE VICTORIAN AND EDWARDIAN TOURIST

A steamer sails out of St Andrews-by-the-Sea in New Brunswick, Canada. British tourists who crossed the Atlantic to explore this coastline would have been surprised to see that the souvenir postcards offered for sale there were printed in Britain.

For visitors to the Welsh coast, regular entertainment included shows by groups of pierrots. Here, Caitlin's Royal Pierrots put on a show.

TRAVELLING IN TIME

A locomotive stands ready to pull a train of double-decker coaches on the popular railway from Swansea to Mumbles in South Wales, c. 1906. Originally using horses to pull the trains, this railway was probably the first passenger-carrying railway in Britain when it opened for passengers in 1807.

making lengthy tours, both in Britain and abroad, what Cook offered was a package holiday designed for, and within the budget of, the middle classes, and even some of the working class.

Coming at a time when holiday entitlements were improving – albeit usually unpaid – the opportunity for anyone to go on a holiday without having to do any of the organisation of transport, hotels, and so on, was hugely attractive. And as many of the early tours used only temperance accommodation, they were considered both socially acceptable and family-friendly.

Publishers, too, were quick to exploit the market opened up by the new breed of tourists, many of whom, as city dwellers, would have had no experience of the countryside, or of the scenic and architectural treasures it contained. Books gently guiding the tourist ingenues about what to look for, and how to respond to the beauty they encountered on their travels, therefore found a ready market.

Photography and the package holiday were made for each other, and over the following decades, as more and more people availed themselves of tours organised by Cook and others, photographers set about providing a steady

15

The Trossachs Hotel was a popular venue for package tours of Scotland long before the end of the nineteenth century. This postcard was sent to William Thomas in August 1909 by 'Ma and Dad', whose tour had stopped there for lunch.

The fine frontage of the Terrace Hotel, Margate.

Visitors arrive in their horse-drawn charabancs at the Inversnaid Hotel at the head of Loch Lomond, c. 1904. This was a regular stopover on Thomas Cook's Trossachs tour. A Hartmann postcard.

stream of new images of Britain's romantic landscape for the tourists to take home with them.

Throughout the 1850s and 1860s the tourist infrastructure was expanded, as was the huge catalogue of photographic prints available for purchase. Three of the biggest publishers of prints were Francis Frith of Reigate, George Washington Wilson of Aberdeen and James Valentine & Sons of Dundee. Between them, their catalogues were so extensive by the 1870s that it was reckoned there was hardly a scenic view of merit of which a photographic print had not been published.

There were, by that time, many established package tours of the Lake District, Scotland and elsewhere available to visitors, and, for the more affluent travellers, Frith, Wilson and Valentine published leather-bound volumes containing views of everywhere which would be visited by the tour party. Associations with Walter Scott invariably dominated the selection of photographs in the Scottish volumes, rugged mountains and lakes those in the English albums. Travellers of more modest means – or perhaps travellers with more initiative – could compile their own albums of views, for a few pence per image, as they went along, buying images from stationers, or from local photographers who augmented income from their usual portrait work by selling scenic views to the market leaders.

With increased visitor numbers, there was a pressing need for more hotel and boarding-house beds. The tradition of renting houses at the seaside,

The tearooms at Pittencrieff Glen in Dunfermline. Even package tours stopped for tea.

THE VICTORIAN AND EDWARDIAN TOURIST

'Passengers from Tayvallich and Loch Swin', from a postcard of c. 1905, showing a group making their way from the steamer pier on Loch Sween up to their hotel.

A handbill for the excursions organised by Thomas Cook for travellers in Switzerland. Included was a visit to the Rigi Railway on Tuesdays; passengers were advised to meet the conductor at the steamer at 10.45 a.m.

already well established since the early nineteenth century, was aimed at those wealthy enough to afford both the time and the cost of spending several weeks by the English coast or in the Scottish Highlands. Newspapers in the 1850s regularly carried large advertisements for shooting lodges and cottages with fishing rights available to rent from 1 August for periods of up to three months, or furnished seaside villas available from early June.

However, the increase in tourist trade did expose a shortage of lower-priced accommodation which could cater for a touring party for just one or two nights at a time. By the end of the century, many small hotels and inns had established an annexe which catered for charabanc or coach parties during the season, and which could be closed off when there was no demand. Such annexes increased in number across the country when motor coaches brought larger and larger groups on scenic tours, and continued to thrive well into the second half of the twentieth century.

Since the 1850s, a common entertainment in the middle-class Victorian drawing room had been the stereoscopic viewer, and until the First World War travellers could purchase stereo views of their favourite places, and enjoy them back at home in all their three-dimensional magic.

18

On the Rigi Mountain Railway: a Photochrom from the 1890s. By 1896 coloured Photochrom prints of all the popular Swiss tourist attractions were available.

Tourists are fickle, however, and despite their admiration of the sepia photographic prints – and the hand-tinted versions of them – which they bought to remind them of their visits, such mementoes were soon considered inadequate. Purchasers and critics lamented the fact that although photography had been in existence for more than fifty years it was still – by the 1890s – unable to celebrate nature in its true colourful glory. So, in 1895, the Photochrom Company of Zürich launched what it claimed were prints by 'real colour photography' – a claim it would be unable to make today, as they clearly were not photographed in colour.

By the summer of 1896 the company's catalogue of views covered most of Europe. Tourists loved them and the prints sold in large numbers. Photochroms were actually black-and-white photographs overprinted by lithography in several colours to look like natural colour, and had it not been for the arrival of the tinted photographic postcard – much cheaper, and also much more useful as a communication medium – they might have enjoyed a longer period of commercial success.

But it was the picture postcard which was to define Edwardian tourism in the days before amateur photography became affordable for most tourists. The tinted postcard especially, printed in Saxony or Bavaria, where the best colour printing was produced, offered tourists a beautiful reminder of their

THE VICTORIAN AND EDWARDIAN TOURIST

'I have been on steamer trips every day as yet,' wrote ARJ to Miss M. Jones, who lived in Gloucestershire, adding 'There are 90 staying at this hotel, I will tell you all about our lively goings-on when I return.' Photographers Philipse & Lees photographed parties setting off from Edwardian Ilfracombe for a sail on the PS *Albion* and had postcards printed and ready to sell to them on their return just a few hours later the same day.

Wrapped up well, tourists descend the Sychnant Pass in North Wales; a 1908 postcard.

experiences, and at a very reasonable price. It was the rare combination of high quality and low price which ensured the postcard's success – that and the rapid adoption of postcard collecting as a pastime.

With postcards, an album of travel memories could be compiled at a fraction of the cost of original photographs, and the range of attractive albums in which to keep the collection safe ranged from the lavish and expensive to the cheap and utilitarian.

So the Edwardian postcard fed two quite distinct markets. The first – as a personal memento of the journey – resulted in the many postcards surviving today which were never posted. They were the Edwardian equivalent of the

TRAVELLING IN TIME

A view of Lucerne, in Switzerland, produced in 1896 by the Photochrom Company of Zürich, and a popular tourist memento. Photochrom prints were produced by multi-colour lithography, with sometimes as many as fourteen different ink colours being applied in sequence to produce what the company claimed was 'natural colour photography'. Photochrom prints can often be found pasted on to the back pages of late-Victorian tourist albums, otherwise filled with the sepia images typical of nineteenth-century travel.

mid-Victorian carte-de-visite, and were sold and preserved in even greater numbers. The sheer range of their subject matter stimulated the collecting craze. Their second market, as a communication medium – they were the Edwardian equivalent of the text message – has left the present-day historian with some delightful insights into the world of the Edwardian tourist through the messages from the senders written on the back.

This Irish postcard of c. 1905 is titled 'Scene at the top of Blarney Castle. Tourist, about to kiss the stone'.

21

Passengers embarking on the 1894-built PS *La Marguerite* at Llandudno for the return trip to Liverpool in the summer of 1908. This elegant 1,500-ton steamer had been built for the Tilbury to Boulogne service, but had proved too expensive to operate. She was sold to the Liverpool & North Wales Steamship Company, where lower wages and cheaper coal made her profitable. It was not unusual for her to carry nearly a thousand passengers for a day trip to Llandudno.

Strictly speaking, these were 'trippers' rather than 'tourists' as they did the round trip in a day. To be identified as a tourist, the traveller had to spend at least one night away from home. That distinction had been made well before the end of the nineteenth century.

MANCHESTER. FIRST EDITION.

HOLIDAY TOURS

SEASON 1902

Organised and Arranged by

THOS. COOK & SON

LUDGATE CIRCUS, LONDON, E.C.

THOMAS COOK'S TOURS

IN A LETTER HOME, written on board the steamer *Espero*, James Ferguson's new wife Elizabeth, known as Eliza, wrote:

> At 10 o'clock at night we all went on board this ship, although it did not sail till 12 o'clock; however, Mr Cook wished us all to be on board, so, like good children, we did his bidding, and getting into our allotted cabins, went quietly off to get settled before the boat started. James and I got a state room which was intended for four people, but as there were not many passengers besides Mr Cook's party they can afford us this, and it is on the whole very comfortable. I have the low berth and James has to mount aloft.

They had been married in Glasgow just twelve days earlier, and this was their wedding tour. James came from a family of Glasgow whisky distillers, so the £128 per person cost of their wedding tour did not perturb them.

It was twenty-four-year-old Mrs Ferguson's first time abroad, and her early letters hint at nervousness. It was also her first voyage, but, despite the poor weather, she survived the Channel crossing without too much discomfort. She was less lucky, however, en route from Trieste to Alexandria on board the Clyde-built *Espero*. 'I was all right while in my bunk yesterday morning, but when I got up to dress it was all over with me, but I won't say anything more about it.'

The date was Sunday 22 February 1874 and, as often happened, their Cook's Tour was being led – or 'conducted', as he preferred – by the indomitable Thomas Cook himself. 'Mr Cook' was, by that time, a hardened traveller with more than a quarter of a century's experience in the business, so the stormy crossing from Trieste would not have troubled him.

After a short stay at the Grosvenor Hotel, the Fergusons had joined their tour party and left London on 14 February, travelling to Paris, where they stayed at the Grand Hotel – mentioned by Eliza as being 'most magnificent' and having '700 bed-rooms'. Then they travelled by train – 'Mr Cook travelled with us, and was in our carriage till we came to Turin, a journey of 24 hours by rail' – and then on to Venice and Trieste. Four Americans joined the party at Corfu, making twenty-two in all, but, as the letter says, the Fergusons were 'the only two Scotchies'.

Thomas Cook single-handedly created the 'package tour' and, some even say, started the modern tourist industry. His vision was extraordinary, and his perseverance, even at times of major setbacks, was exceptional. Lesser men might have given up their dream, but Thomas's tenacity apparently knew no

Opposite:
The cover of one of Thomas Cook's 1902 brochures highlights some of the sights to be enjoyed on an Italian tour.

THE VICTORIAN AND EDWARDIAN TOURIST

Right: Thomas's son, John Mason Cook, with his wife, Emma, and their son Frank, who would join him in the family business.

Far right: Thomas Cook, the father of the package holiday, photographed in 1864.

Princes Street, Edinburgh, looking towards Calton Hill, a Photochrom print from c.1897. Centre right in the picture can be seen Thomas Cook's Edinburgh offices.

The carte-de-visite was the ubiquitous tourist memento widely available across Europe for nearly thirty years from 1860. Photography's first standard format enabled tourists to keep the reminders of their tours safely together in the family album.

26

limits, and drove him, and later his son, to build up and operate the largest and most complex travel business in the world. From humble beginnings to global presence took a surprisingly short period of time.

Thomas Cook was apprenticed as a woodturner from the age of thirteen or fourteen, before becoming a Baptist lay preacher and then a printer. He ran a temperance boarding house with his wife in Market Harborough from the late 1830s, and another in Leicester from 1842, and later became a hotelier from 1853 as owner of Cook's Temperance Hotel, before embarking on his dream of becoming an excursion organiser, and later a tour organiser. By the close of the nineteenth century 'tourist' was becoming a pejorative term again, so his customers became known as 'travellers'.

The Midland Railway gave him letters of introduction to help him organise his early tours. One of their directors was Joseph Paxton, designer of the Crystal Palace, so there was plenty of enthusiasm to help Cook organise excursions to London to visit the 1851 Great Exhibition.

Six years earlier, in 1845, Thomas Cook had organised his first tour to Liverpool and the North Wales coast and, starting out as he meant to carry on, to inform his travellers he published the world's first tour guide, *The Tourist's Guide: a Hand Book of the Trip from Leicester, Nottingham and Derby to Liverpool and the Coast of North Wales*. It bears the imprimatur 'Printed by T Cook, 26, Granby Street, Leicester', and for many years subsequently Thomas did all his own printing. In the introduction he wrote:

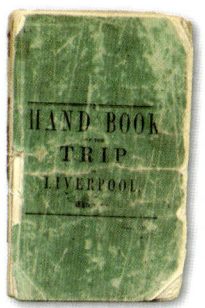

The Tourist's Guide: a Hand Book of the Trip from Leicester, Nottingham and Derby to Liverpool and the Coast of North Wales was the world's first handbook designed for a package tour.

> The announcement of a Railway Trip from Leicester, Nottingham, and Derby, to Liverpool has excited an interest in these parts which has scarcely a parallel in the annals of Special Pleasure Trains; and there is no doubt but great numbers will avail themselves of the opportunity afforded by the liberal Directors of the Midland Company, to view the great Sea port and other places of interest which may be visited from Liverpool. With the view of assisting the tourists in the most economical disposal of their time and means, this little Guide is published, in which the Compiler has endeavoured to point out the various objects of interest on the route, in Liverpool, &c. Parties will have to be 'wide awake' at an early hour, or they will be disappointed.

The train travelled via Leeds and Manchester to Liverpool's Edge Hill station, where 'the passengers are to be set down, special trains not being allowed to pass through the tunnel to the more central station'.

Cook was a pioneer and visionary. His vision was almost complete from the start. Even something as basic as persuading three separate railway companies to accept a single ticket had never been done – and did not

Right: Caernarfon Castle and docks, photographed by Francis Bedford c. 1865. A visit to the town was an option on Cook's first tour to Liverpool and North Wales.

Above: A strip of hotel coupons from 1902. Similar sets were available for all Thomas Cook's travellers to purchase from 1868.

become commonplace until nationalisation of the railways more than a century later.

Passengers were then advised – using Cook's recommendations later in the book – to arrange accommodation and, for those who 'purpose visiting the Welsh Coast', advice was given on acquiring tickets for the steam packet *Eclipse*, which had been specially chartered for the voyage. Other steam packet companies had, apparently, refused to offer him sufficient discount, but 'The proprietor of the *Eclipse*', wrote Cook, 'has evinced a spirit of great urbanity and liberality, and pledges himself that no effort of his shall be spared to render the trip agreeable'. He even 'intimated

An unknown photographer's study of the ivy-covered ruins of Beaumaris Castle, c. 1865. Disembarking from the *Eclipse* to visit the town and castle was an option on Cook's first tour to Liverpool and North Wales.

THOMAS COOK'S TOURS

The North Euston Hotel at Fleetwood, built by the Midland Railway.

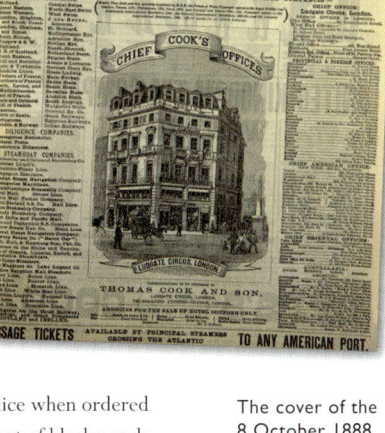

The cover of the 8 October 1888 edition of *Cook's Excursionist and Home and Foreign Tourist Advertiser*.

his intention of having her re-painted and well cleaned for the occasion'.

Included in the itinerary was an opportunity to climb Snowdon, and the entire trip, starting 'from St George's Pier Head, Liverpool, at eight o'clock on Tuesday morning', included opportunities to land at Beaumaris, Bangor, Menai Bridge or Caernarfon. The price was 4s, whether on deck or in the cabin.

As a cautionary tale for anyone visiting Liverpool, Cook quoted from the *Liverpool Albion* of 16 October 1843:

On Friday, Mr Rushton ordered a fellow, who, it was stated, was one of a gang of desperadoes who usually infest the Railway Station, in Lime-street, and are known under the cognomen of 'man-catchers', to pay 10s and costs, for having resisted the police when ordered to move off. It appeared that the prisoner was one of a knot of blackguards who are in the habit of blocking the gateway at the Station, where they are continually on the look-out for strangers, whom, as soon as they set foot on ground, they importune and nearly drag out of their habiliments, under the pretence of finding them comfortable lodgings. The object is apparent – these scamps have a commission from certain low crimps in the town for bringing strangers to their domiciles. Once in the hands of these cormorants, an embargo is set upon their persons or their luggage, and it is seldom they have the chance to extricate themselves before they have been made to pay dearly for their whistles.

29

James Valentine's idyllic study of Swan Island in Loch Lomond, from the 1870s. A sail on the loch featured in Cook's earliest Scottish tours, on board the steamers *Loch Lomond* and *Waterwitch*.

Aberfoyle had been a stopping place on Cook's Scottish tours almost from their introduction in 1846. Here, coaches leave the Bailie Nichol Jarvie Hotel, c. 1906, for the journey to Loch Katrine, a route which, by that time, Cook's tourists had been following for sixty years.

In the book, Cook listed good temperance hotels, including the Liverpool Temperance Hotel, Johnston's, Cottom's, Joseph Jones's and Spurrs. Hotels in Menai Bridge, Caernarfon and Bangor were also recommended, as well as 'good inns' elsewhere, and his own Temperance Boarding House in Leicester for the night before the journey.

These were still the days before photographs were available for tourists to buy, so anyone on the tour wishing to take home a memento of their visit would have purchased an engraving or a sketch. The market for tourist photographs was still a decade and a half in the future when Cook's party set out for Liverpool and North Wales.

The Handbook of a Trip to Scotland was published in the following year, 1846, as an accompaniment to the first tour north of the border. In the

THOMAS COOK'S TOURS

introduction, Cook summed up his ideals for the traveller:

> Travelling should incite to a warmer and more enduring patriotism. The depth of the 'amour patriae' is never fully disclosed till we see the misty lines of our native hills recede, or after long absence thrill with ecstasy, as they gleam upon the horizon, like the wings of a guardian angel.

And, later, he wrote of the itinerary he had arranged: 'It must be a splendid affair; such a gathering as has never been convened on any similar occasion.'

It turned out not to be quite as splendid as he originally envisaged. Plans for a daytime voyage from Fleetwood to Ardrossan on the specially chartered PS (paddle steamer) *Falcon*, which he had hoped to fill with 1,200 to 1,400 passengers, had to be abandoned when only 350 tourists signed up for that first tour. The journey was therefore undertaken overnight on a scheduled steam packet with inadequate cabin accommodation – and a very wet night it was too. The pages of descriptions of what might have been seen on the voyage up the Scottish coast counted for nothing. It was wet, the sea was rough, and it was dark. So it was a very bedraggled and somewhat disgruntled party which stepped off the steamer and on to the waiting Glasgow train.

From Glasgow they travelled to Edinburgh, which at the time had no direct rail link with England, but, wrote Cook:

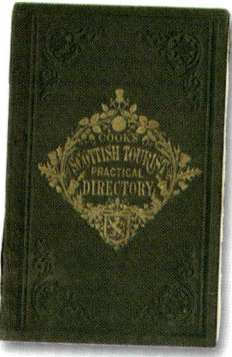

Cook's Scottish Tourist Practical Directory, one of the company's many Victorian handbooks.

Cook's first Scottish tour, while including voyages on Lochs Lomond and Long, did not include Loch Katrine, where a paddle-steamer service on the *Gypsy* had been introduced in 1843. By 1845, a more powerful paddle-steamer, the *Rob Roy*, was launched, to be replaced in the 1850s by a screw-driven steamer of the same name, seen here in a late 1860s photograph by James Valentine. Cook's tours included a trip on the *Rob Roy* from 1847.

31

The cover of the June 1892 edition of *Cook's Excursionist*.

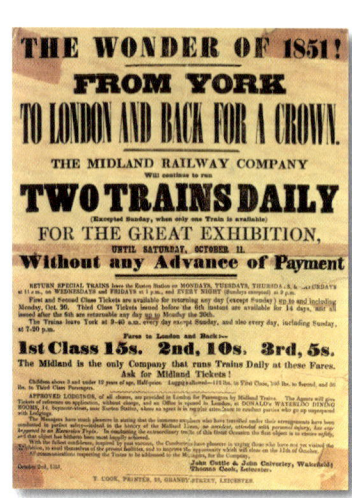

A flyer advertising trips to the Great Exhibition, 1851.

There is however one line on the eve of completion, which will connect the Northern with the Southern Metropolis; viz, the North British Railway, which unites with the Edinburgh and Glasgow by a Junction at the North Bridge where a Grand Central Station will soon be formed.

That 'Grand Central Station' would become Edinburgh Waverley.

At both Edinburgh and Glasgow soirées were arranged so that the tourists could meet 'warm-hearted' locals, and two evening entertainments by 'the Hutchinson Family' had also been arranged in Scotland's capital, as were steamer trips on Loch Lomond and Loch Long.

So, in that very first Scottish tour, Cook had identified and organised many of the enduring and staple ingredients of the package holiday – transport, entertainment, excursions, tour management and guides, and opportunities to engage with local people.

The recipe for a successful tour was in place right from the start.

By 1855, with his British tours embracing almost the entire country, Cook ventured across the Channel with his first two trips to Belgium, Germany and France. Neither made money, but he was undaunted by such setbacks.

Ten years later, with an office now established in London, Thomas was arranging tours across the United States – travelling the routes himself, selecting hotels, railway companies and places to visit, while his son, John Mason Cook, stayed at home and ran the business. Thomas was the impresario and visionary, the hands-on conductor, while John was the businessman – a separation in ideals which would ultimately drive them apart in 1878.

But before then he had conquered Egypt, chartering two steamers in February 1869 to take his first tour up the Nile. He was again in Egypt in November 1869, on the occasion of the opening of the Suez Canal.

In the pages of *Cook's Excursionist*, Thomas advertised a 60-guinea ticket to Egypt, which was to include attendance at the opening of the canal on 17 November 1869. There were few takers, however, so he suggested an alternative tour by steamer and train to Brindisi, and then by steamer to Alexandria, at a price of £35 first class, or £28 second class, leaving his tourists to book their own accommodation. In the end he limited himself to taking a few friends with him and, to avoid paying the excessive prices being asked for hotels – £2 8s per day, his party lived on board their steamer. They did, however, take part in the inaugural procession along the canal, an experience which Thomas later described as one of the highlights of his life.

Only five years after that first foray into Egypt, Cook's Egyptian tours were world renowned, and there were more Americans than British in the 1874 party with which the Fergusons travelled through France and Italy to Cairo, and on to the Holy Land.

The origins of *Cook's Excursionist and Tourist Advertiser*, Thomas's periodical which advertised and promoted all his tours, could be traced back to 1851, just six years after Thomas's first tour to Liverpool. It first appeared as *Cook's Exhibition Herald and Excursion Advertiser* on 31 May 1851 and contained advance notice of the first of many excursions to London and the Great Exhibition.

'The conductor of the HERALD', wrote Thomas in the first issue, 'has spent a good portion of ten summers in catering for the gratification of the travelling public, and his highest reward has been the satisfaction, gratification and appreciation of his patrons and friends.'

Among the souvenirs of the Great Exhibition on sale to tourists were stereoscopic daguerreotypes of the exhibits by some of the leading photographers of the day.

An engraving of the interior of the Crystal Palace in Hyde Park, based on a photograph by J. J. E. Mayall. Cook's many excursions to the Great Exhibition brought over 150,000 visitors to London.

THE VICTORIAN AND EDWARDIAN TOURIST

Below: A return ticket for an excursion in 1877

Bottom: The ideal postcard for tourists in Switzerland, showing the viewing area at Neisen Kulm, 2,387 metres above sea level in the Bernese Alps, and identifying the major peaks in view: the Schreckhorn, 4,080 metres; the Eiger, 3,975 metres; the Monch, 4,104 metres; and the Jungfrau, 4,166 metres. Cook's first Swiss tour was organised in 1863.

In addition to Cook's planned trips, the *Herald* contained several pages of advertisements for hotels and other accommodation in London. Readers were advised:

W. Scrimshaw, from Leicester but many years a resident in London, has been induced in compliance with the wishes of friends, to open a PRIVATE HOTEL AND BOARDING HOUSE, where Economy consistent with Respectability and Comfort will be obtained. 28 Upper Stamford Street, Waterloo Bridge Road. Omnibuses to and from the Exhibition every three minutes.

Cook's clientele in those early days came predominantly from the Leicester and Derby areas, so Mr Scrimshaw's Leicester credentials were clearly helpful.

But Cook was keen that everyone should have the opportunity to visit the exhibition for its educational value, whatever their social background. A separate entry advertised:

LODGINGS FOR THE WORKING CLASSES DURING THE EXHIBITION OF 1851. Accommodation is provided for 200 men at one time. The sleeping apartments are fitted up in the same style as Emigrants' Ships. Each man has a berth to himself, a flock bed, pillow, one blanket, two sheets, coverlet – all clean. Accommodation for washing, with towels, and other conveniences; and the use of plates, knives and forks, together with attendance, will be supplied. H. Castle & Co., Baltic Wharf, Millbank, Westminster.

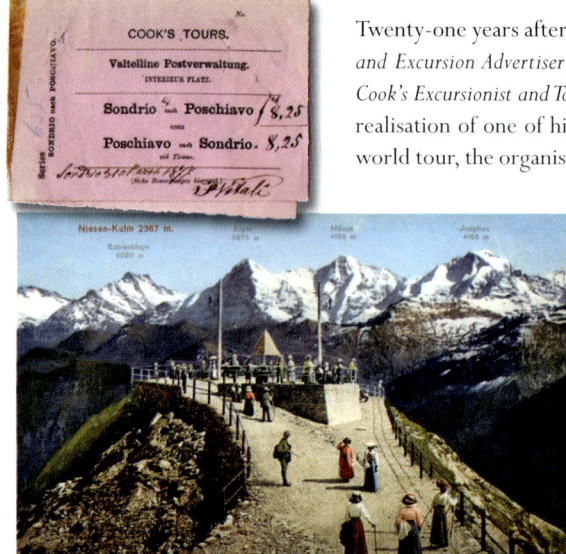

Twenty-one years after the first issue of *Cook's Exhibition Herald and Excursion Advertiser*, Thomas was able to use the pages of *Cook's Excursionist and Tourist Advertiser* in 1872 to announce the realisation of one of his greatest ambitions – the first Cook's world tour, the organisation of which must have stretched him to the limit.

He was, by that time, sixty-three years of age, and, while his son John ran the business, Thomas still liked to check out in person every new venture he initiated. The world tour, and his other commitments in Egypt, meant that from September 1872 he spent 222 days away from home.

The world tour went on to become an annual event, but the first one involved organisation on a scale never before attempted. The party sailed from Liverpool to New York, crossed the United States by several different railway companies to San Francisco, before taking another steamer to Japan and then China. They continued on to Singapore, Ceylon (Sri Lanka) and India, then Cairo, after which most continued on home through Europe. Thomas, however, had already committed to conducting an extended tour through Egypt and the Holy Land, returning through Turkey, Greece, Italy and France.

A major step forward in the success of the package tour had been introduced four years earlier when Cook's extended their pricing structure to include the cost of hotel rooms and meals. The introduction of their hotel vouchers made their tours truly 'all-inclusive' – except for drinks, of course, which were always excluded. Six years later, in 1874, the company introduced 'Cook's Circular Note' in New York, and another of the essential and enduring features of international travel was in place – the traveller's cheque.

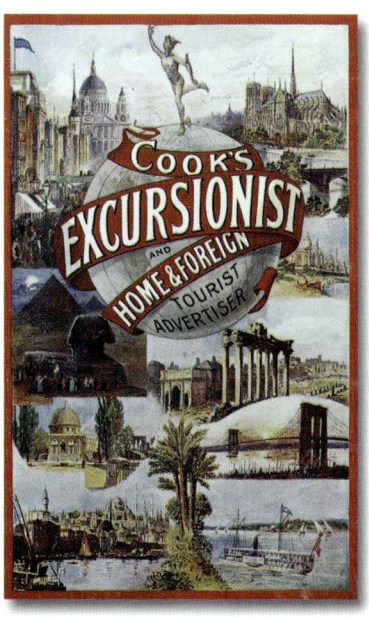

Establishing and maintaining this enormous and complex network of routes required a monumental amount of work on the part of both Thomas and John Mason Cook. While Thomas planned every new route by making the journey himself – travelling tens of thousands of miles in doing so – John travelled even further.

He was the businessman, the one who set up Cook's offices in countries thousands of miles away from the company's London base, and made sure they were properly managed, and the staff properly trained. According to Fraser Rae, in his 1891 book *The Business of Travel*, John travelled between 42,000 and 53,000 miles annually between 1865 and 1873. From 1873 until 1880, he seems to have been even busier, travelling 'with little intermission' throughout Europe and the United States. Exhausted by his incessant railway travelling, especially by night in an age before sleeping cars, he eventually decided to cut back on rail journeys, and to travel, whenever possible, by sea instead. For the remainder of his life – he died in 1899 – John spent every winter in either Egypt, Palestine or India.

Thomas Cook & Son had gone from being, in effect, a one-man business in 1845 to a global concern in little over a quarter of a century. It was a remarkable achievement, but John's more commercial approach was at odds with his father's enduring fascination with the romance of travel.

The *Excursionist* was given a colour cover from 1900.

Cook's European guide from 1865, two years after the first Swiss tour.

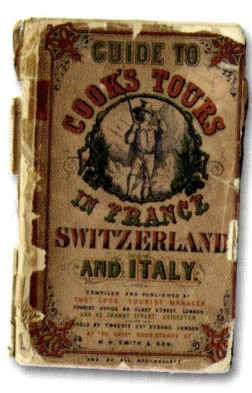

THE VICTORIAN AND EDWARDIAN TOURIST

  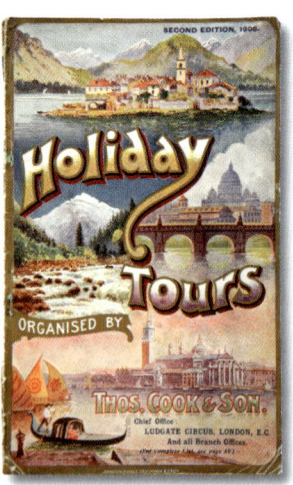

The colourful covers of three of Cook's annual publications from the Edwardian era – *Holiday Tours* from 1901, 1906 and 1908.

The Nile Steamer *Tewfik*.

Despite their continuing partnership, the two men's relationship was strained almost to breaking point, and their partnership finally came to an end in 1878. The rift was apparently so deep that they were never reconciled, and Thomas never saw his grandchildren, apart from Frank. Under John's leadership, however, Thomas Cook & Son continued to grow, continued to extend its network of routes, and to define the package tourist industry.

From small beginnings, the American business grew rapidly, with tours to Europe and Egypt from the United States proving even more popular than tours from Europe to the United States; in several catalogues, the globe is centred on the Americas, and the featured locations are in the 'old world' rather than the new.

By the mid-1880s John had organised the construction of Cook's own fleet of Nile steamers – the most luxurious on the river – and business was growing substantially year on year.

Father and son, however, were both exhausted. Thomas died in July 1892, at the age of eighty-three, and his son John just seven years later, in March 1899, at the age of sixty-five. The company was, by that time, being run by his sons Frank, Ernest and Thomas (known as Bert). Only nine years after the end of the Edwardian era, Cook's became the first travel agent in the world to offer pleasure trips by air. Their legacy endures to this day.

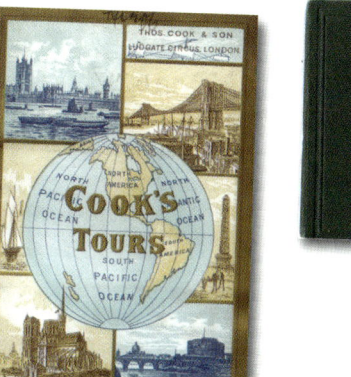

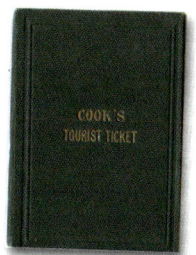

'Montreal, The Quay', with the huge paddle-wheeler *Quebec*, built in Glasgow in 1864, which sailed the St Laurence River. This postcard shows her after 1907, when she was lengthened and fitted with a second funnel.

Tourist coaches loading outside postcard stores in Ria Juana, Mexico, 1909.

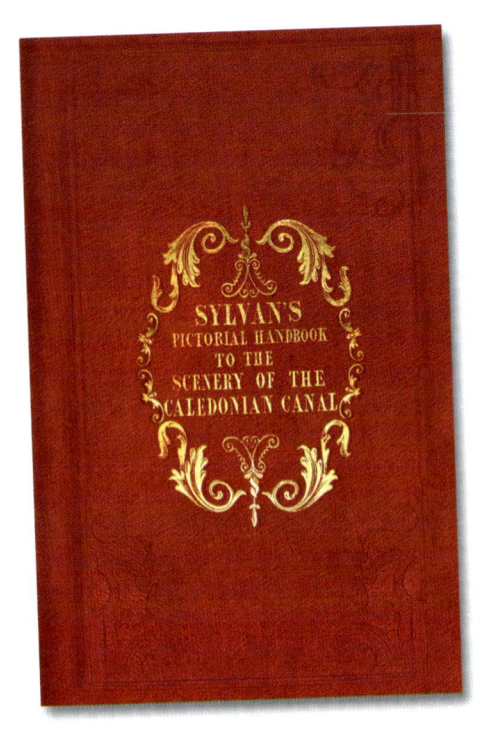

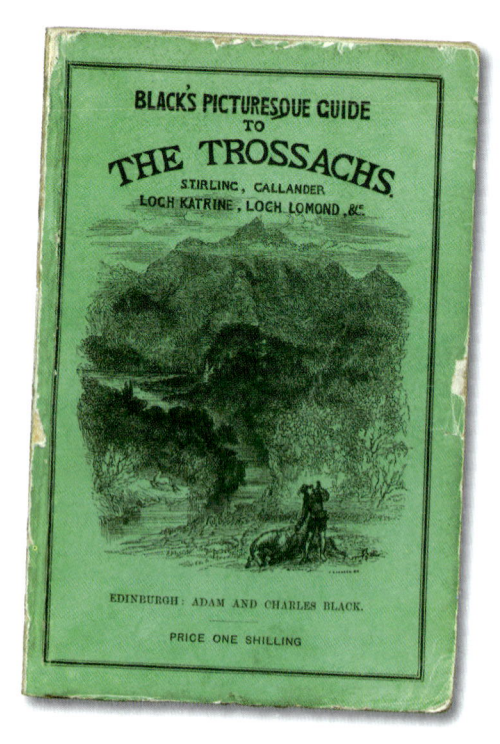

Above: Among the early Scottish guidebooks were *Sylvan's Pictorial Handbook to the Scenery of the Caledonian Canal* and *Black's Picturesque Guide to the Trossachs*.

Guidebooks to North Wales all recommended the coach trip through the Sychnant Pass near Penmaenmawr.

THE UBIQUITOUS GUIDEBOOK

LONG BEFORE the development of the tourist industry, writers had been producing what we would today describe as 'travelogues'. The first attempt at writing a comprehensive guide to Britain can be traced back as far as 1577, when William Camden started work on *Britannia*, published in 1586. Despite being written in Latin, it proved very popular, running to six editions by 1607.

Several notable works, which can be seen as the direct predecessors of guidebooks, were published in the eighteenth century, among them Daniel Defoe's acclaimed three-volume work published in 1724, *A Tour Thro' the Whole Island of Great Britain*. Just three years after publishing *Robinson Crusoe*, he had embarked on a project about as different as could be from his story of life on a desert island.

Defoe's book mixes astute observation with factual description and, although he moved from one country house to the next as he travelled the country, some of his accounts are vividly descriptive of eighteenth-century Britain. In Bridport, Dorset, he noted: 'Such was the plenty of fish that year, that mackerell, the finest and largest I ever saw, were sold at the sea side a hundred for a penny.'

Upper Bow, Edinburgh, James Valentine, c. 1870. Tourists in Edinburgh could buy *Black's Guide through Edinburgh with Pleasure Excursions in the Environs*, published in 1850, which took them around the city in a series of planned walks. Architectural descriptions were interlaced with stories of the city's sometimes macabre past, and anecdotes about famous past residents.

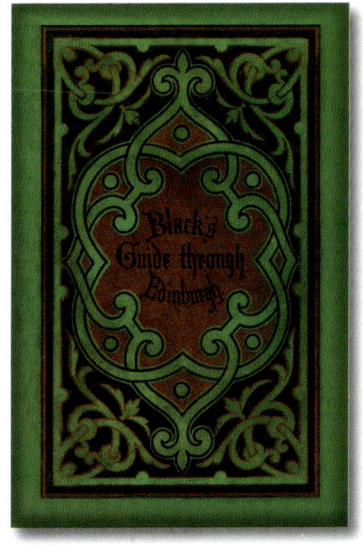

THE VICTORIAN AND EDWARDIAN TOURIST

A group of visitors to Edinburgh Castle, c. 1904, viewing Mons Meg (middle background), a massive cannon which fired balls 50 cm in diameter. A guided tour of the castle was one of the highlights of a visit to Scotland from the earliest days of Cook's tours. The visit was often timed to coincide with the firing of the time gun at 1 p.m. each day. Mons Meg was made in 1449 for Philip, Duke of Burgundy.

Defoe's *Tour* was not intended as a guidebook as we know it today, although it did set out to offer

…useful observations [on the] Principal Cities and Towns, their Situation, Magnitude, Government and Commerce; The Customs, Manners, Speech, as also the Exercises, Diversions, and Employment of the People; The Produce and Improvement of the Lands, the Trade, and Manufacture [and] The Public Edifices, Seats, and Palaces of the NOBILITY and GENTRY.

Almost fifty years later, Thomas Pennant published a two-volume account of his two extensive tours of Scotland, undertaken in 1769 and 1772. Travel-writing in those days was a relatively unsophisticated art, so Pennant's

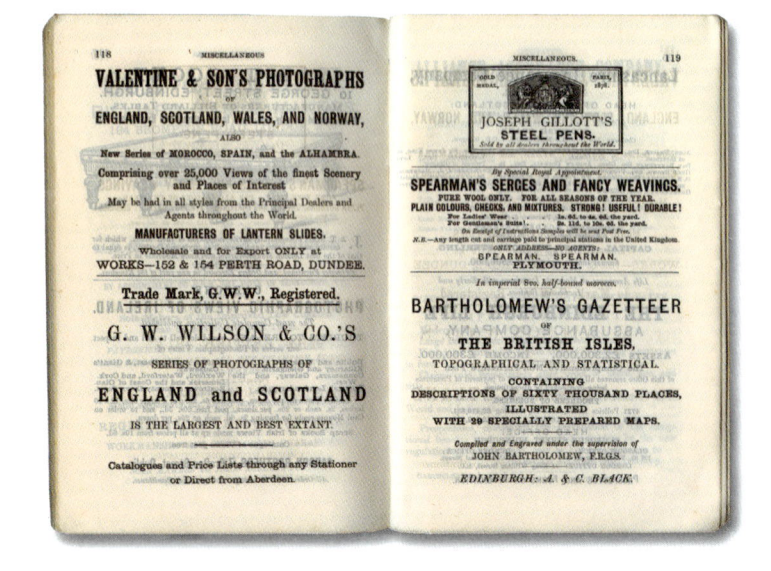

Many guidebooks included advertisements for maps and for the leading photographers of the day.

40

THE UBIQUITOUS GUIDEBOOK

account is not in the lyrical vein we expect of guides today, but it does offer a unique and sometimes insightful view of the country. His writing style is very much in the vein of the tourist pocket guides which would start to appear in the middle of the nineteenth century, guiding his readers along the way, and telling them what to expect. He described what he saw in vivid word pictures. Travel then was not easy, and always slow, but Pennant's perseverance rarely waned, nor did his enthusiasm for the scenery and people he encountered.

Whereas Defoe was concerned with the great houses, the great men and the great manufacturers of Britain, Pennant was fascinated by Scotland's landscape, and the history which had been played out on that landscape. Throughout his travels, he is clearly writing about his first-hand experiences, as well as offering an early guidebook for visitors to Scotland.

After visiting Dunvegan Castle on the Isle of Skye, Pennant revelled in the fact:

> Am lodged this night in the same bed that formerly received the unfortunate Charles Stuart. Here he lay one night, after having been for some time in a female habit under the protection of Flora Macdonald

— a tangible link with the history of Scotland's relatively recent turbulent past which so fascinated him.

In Victorian and Edwardian times trains from London to the Lakes and Scotland on the West Coast Main Line all passed through Carnforth station in Lancashire. The station was opened in 1846 by the Lancaster & Carlisle Railway Company and originally had just a single platform, but extensive reconstruction in the 1880s under the London & North Western Railway provided a main platform 300 yards long.

Cambridge station, c. 1905. At the platform stands a Great Eastern Railway 4-4-0 locomotive. Opened by the Eastern Counties Railway in 1845, and greatly expanded and rebuilt in 1896 and again in 1908, Cambridge became a major interchange for tourists travelling from London into eastern England.

Half a century later, the first proper guidebooks aimed at the growing number of tourists to the country would start to appear. In 1847 the anonymous author of *Sylvan's Pictorial Handbook to the Clyde and Its Watering Places* wrote that:

> The fame of the Scottish Lochs, and of
> > Their islands that, empurpled bright,
> > Float there amid the livelier light;
> > And mountains that like giants stand,
> > To sentinel enchanted land
>
> has spread wherever the 'well of English undefiled' of Sir Walter Scott has made a channel for itself; and scarcely less familiar has been the great Scottish river, the highway to the rare and gorgeous scenery he has painted; while those who have hitherto known the country only from description, may now, by the aid of the rapid railway and steamboat, within a week or two, explore it for themselves: for in less than four and twenty hours, the traveller from England may find himself amidst those renowned solitudes.

This sort of florid language was typical of early British tourist guides, designed to do much more than simply describe locations. For a society largely unused to exploring and enjoying either landscape or heritage, the writers of early guides saw their role as creating word pictures designed to

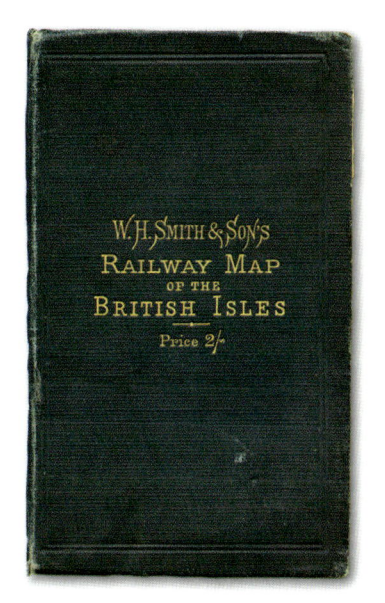

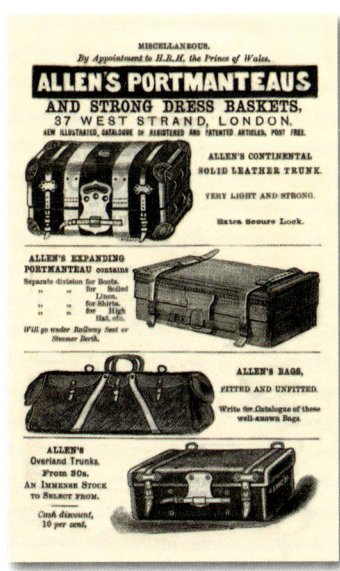

Left: Priced at 2s in the 1880s, W. H. Smith's *Railway Map of the British Isles* was not cheap. But, with it, tourists and travellers could make their way across Britain's very complex railway network. W. H. Smith's were to be found in just about every station and, armed with the map and a railway timetable, the tourist was free to explore.

Right: In addition to carrying selected railway timetables, most Victorian guidebooks carried pages of advertisements for hotels, coach operators, and luggage fit for an independent tourist. Even in the nineteenth century, space could be minimal, so several companies advertised portmanteaus which 'will go under railway seat or steamer berth'.

encourage travel, to romanticise both the landscape and the idea of travel, and to create an almost magical expectation among their readers – many of whom would read their guidebooks *en route* on the train.

The popularity of the writings of Sir Walter Scott, and Queen Victoria's enthusiasm for the romantic landscape of Scotland, both encouraged Scotland's emerging tourist industry. Scott's novels and poetry had introduced the magic of the Highland landscape to a large percentage of the population, and now, with easier travel, there was the wherewithal to capitalise on that popularity.

Surprisingly, the identity of 'Sylvan' has remained a mystery. Indeed, he or she might have been several different people, and the pseudonym simply a device adopted by the publisher, John Johnstone of Paternoster Row, London. Johnstone was more used to publishing religious tracts and treatises, so the diversification into travel guides was a new area of publishing for him.

The handbook to the Clyde was published alongside *Sylvan's Pictorial Handbook to the English Lakes*, and Johnstone's advertisements at the back of both books make it clear that an extensive series of tourist guides was planned – among the first illustrated pocket guidebooks published in Britain. Tourism was rapidly becoming big business, and Johnstone was keen to establish his place in this growing market.

Plans were already in hand in 1847 to add *Sylvan's Pictorial Handbook to the Isle of Arran, Sylvan's Pictorial Handbook to Loch Lomond, Loch Katrine and the Trosachs* [sic], *Sylvan's Pictorial Handbook to the Land o' Burns* and *Sylvan's Pictorial*

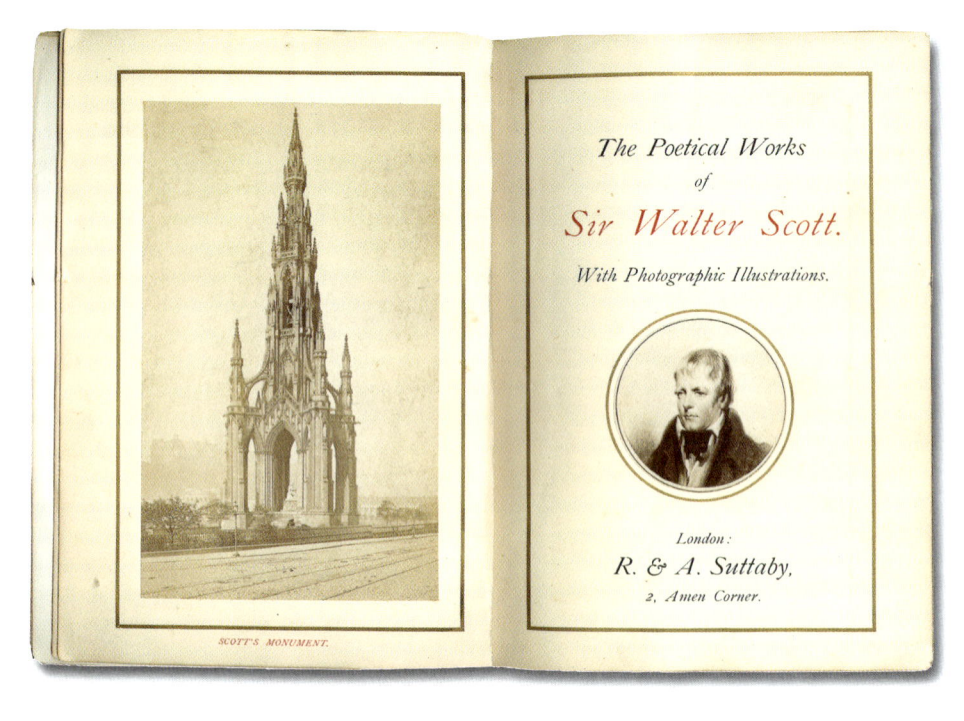

For wealthy tourists, photographically illustrated books were available from the 1860s. James Valentine sold albums of photographs of all the sites on a Scottish tour, while several publishers offered volumes of Scott's work, illustrated with real photographs.

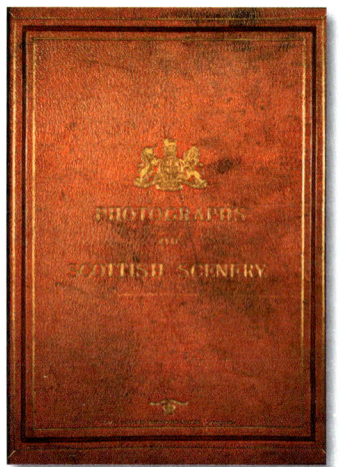

Handbook to the Scenery of the Caledonian Canal. The last two titles appeared in the following year, 1848, but searches have so far failed to locate the planned guides to Arran and the Trossachs. Perhaps they never made it into print. The writer continued:

Thus, from Liverpool, which is the great steam-boat starting point to the Clyde and the Scottish lochs, we may reach Greenock in about fourteen hours: but, whether the tourist proceed from London or by the North Western route from the midland counties, over the great iron roads of Yorkshire and Northumberland, and by way of Edinburgh to Glasgow, or whether he start from a more northerly port, he will arrive at his destination in an equally brief space of time.

If our tourists were on a package trip, then they would carry with them hotel vouchers for their overnight stays. If, however, they were travelling independently, then the advertising sections included at the back of most guidebooks after the 1850s were essential reading – for they contained hotel advertisements for just about every location along the increasingly well-worn tourist trail. Regularly served by coaches, these hotels were ideal 'watering places' for the weary traveller.

Many hotels, for example, advertised that they would collect visitors from the nearest steamer pier, or from railway stations, and transport them to their destinations. They also offered to book coach journeys to the major sights of the area, book coastal or river steamer trips, and so on. For those planning to stop for more than a night or two, fishing permits could be obtained – their price often included as part of the cost of staying at the hotel.

Johnstone's parent company, Longman, Brown, Green & Longmans, was also in the marketplace. Their delightfully titled 1848 publication *Miss Costello's North Wales*, subtitled *The Falls, Lakes and Mountains of North Wales*,

> ...indicates the most picturesque features of some of the most beautiful scenery in Europe; it tells the history and traditions of the most remarkable sites; and, independently of painting the charms of this romantic region in language full of harmony and colour it presents to the eye a profusion of sketches whose truth and vigour and delicacy of execution are worthy of the highest commendation.

The locomotive *Snowdon* – an 0-4-2 tank engine built in 1896 by the Swiss Locomotive & Manufacturing Co of Winterthur – stands at Clogwyn, the second highest station on the Snowdon Mountain Railway, while another train makes its way down from the summit. *Snowdon* is still operational today. The Snowdon Railway, opened in 1896, remains the only rack and pinion railway in Britain and is still a magnet for tourists.

45

Bookstalls at major railway stations such as Newcastle stocked a wide range of maps, timetables and guidebooks for travellers. By the time this postcard was published c.1905, W. H. Smith & Sons had bookstalls in stations from London to the Scottish border, and their range would have included their own maps and guides, as well as the latest edition of Bradshaw's *Railway Companion*.

As travel became more widespread, and the railway network expanded, the tourist might also arm himself with an up-to-date railway map – those published by Phillips and by W. H. Smith were the best known – and use that together with his guidebooks to plan his itinerary. He might also obtain a copy of Bradshaw's railway timetables to facilitate his passage across the country.

George Bradshaw published his first timetable in Manchester on 19 October 1839 – the world's first comprehensive railway timetable. It cost 6d and was titled *Bradshaw's Railway Time Tables and Assistant to Railway Travelling*. Later editions were called *Bradshaw's Railway Companion* and were much larger. From eight pages in 1839 – when there were still very few railways – Bradshaw had grown to nearly one thousand pages by the end of the nineteenth century. In 1865 *Punch* magazine praised *Bradshaw's Railway Companion*, saying that 'seldom has the gigantic intellect of man been employed upon a work of greater utility'.

As a spin-off from the growing popularity of both guidebooks and travel, there was a huge potential market for books illustrated with real photographs rather than engravings. Their production, however, remained prohibitively expensive until the end of the nineteenth century. Nonetheless, travellers to Scotland in the 1870s in search of memories of Sir Walter Scott were, in some numbers, apparently willing to pay for illustrated volumes of Scott's works. But photographically illustrated guidebooks would remain a dream for decades.

The problem was combining high quality with low cost – Black's *Picturesque Guides*, for example, cost only a shilling, and that ruled photography out. For more expensive productions, with a much higher cover price, cost would prove to be much less of an issue, and would lead to the introduction of what we know today as 'coffee-table' books.

The pioneer in the publication of coffee-table books was Walter Bentley Woodbury, who had invented a process for the mechanical mass-production of photographs. Before Woodbury's process, photographically illustrated books required real photographs to be pasted onto the pages, but his carbon-pigment printing process yielded mechanically printed illustrations with most of the subtlety of original photographic prints.

Treasure Spots of the World was published in 1875 by Ward, Lock & Tyler – another publisher in London's Paternoster Row. In his introduction, Woodbury wrote that:

> The object of this, the first gift-book of its character, is to place before the public a selection of the most celebrated of the world's beauties and wonders, which all being pictures of the unerring sun's work, are necessarily true to the places they represent, without flattery.

Even then, the idea that 'the camera cannot lie' was well embedded into the public mind.

The book was designed for the armchair traveller, and contained twenty-eight beautifully printed photographic plates with accompanying descriptive

The Swiss were already highly skilled at building and operating mountain railways on steep inclines. Their engines originally used vertical boilers – as seen here descending Mount Rigi in the 1870s – and they subsequently pioneered a design using inclined boilers, as at Snowdon, to ensure the engine did not run dry while climbing the mountain. Snowdon's locomotives always ascend the mountain funnel first.

THE VICTORIAN AND EDWARDIAN TOURIST

Below: Niagara River in Winter', by Charles Bierstadt, from *Treasure Spots of the World*, was accompanied by an essay by Walter Bentley Woodbury, who wrote: 'Niagara! What magic is the name to all of us; how few of us have realized its actual glories, yet how few but have drawn some picture of its grandeur in our imaginations.'

Below right: Woodbury's own study of the colossal figure at Singa-Sarie on Java was taken while he was living on the island.

texts. The photographs had been taken by some of the world's leading photographers – including Adolphe Braun and John Thomson – and covered locations from Tintern Abbey to Niagara Falls, from Java to Seville. It was produced to the very highest production standards, and could even be purchased in a range of different coloured covers.

If Woodbury made a mistake, it was in allowing some of the photographers to write the texts accompanying their pictures. Of Weggis on Lake Lucerne, the photographer, Stephen Thomson, wrote:

> When the returning Spring shall make the meadows green, the leaves burst forth anew, and the warm sun spread 'a light of laughing flowers' along its banks, and aged people and stunted cretins creep forth to bask in the unwonted ray, Weggis will awaken also, for Weggis is the place of embarkation for travellers returning from the Rigi. Its whilome deserted quay will swarm with tourists of all nations, presenting every variety of costume, many of them carrying alpenstocks crowned with turfs of the sweet-scented alpine rose.

– not the prose we would expect from a travelogue today.

The changing character and use of language is always fascinating. When the second edition of Baedeker's *Guide to Great Britain: A Handbook for Travellers* was published in 1890, it was proudly announced that the book had been revised, expanded and 'brought down to date'. The introduction continued:

48

The Editor has endeavoured to enumerate, not only the first class hotels, but others also of more modest pretensions, which may be safely selected by the 'voyageur en garçon', with little sacrifice of comfort and great saving of expenditure.

Even in the 1890s, inflation was clearly an issue, for Baedeker's writer – the Scots-born J. F. Muirhead MA – went on to observe that 'Although changes frequently take place, and prices generally have an upward tendency, the average charges stated in the Handbook will enable the traveller to form a fair estimate of his expenditure.'

James Muirhead, with his brother Findlay, would later acquire the publishing rights for John Murray's travel guides, and in 1918 establish their own 'Blue Guides' series, following in the finest tradition of nineteenth-century tourist handbooks.

Baedeker, however, was not just for those in search of the scenic and picturesque: it made more than a passing reference to industrial life, and thus gives us a useful snapshot of the country in late Victorian times. The book quickly became one of the most popular tourist guides in Britain, although it was not always complimentary. Newcastle, for example, according to James Muirhead, was a 'somewhat dingy town' of 150,000 inhabitants, best-known for its 'large ship-building yards and manufactories of locomotives and iron goods'. Its adjacent coalfields, he said, made it 'one of the chief coal-exporting ports of Great Britain'.

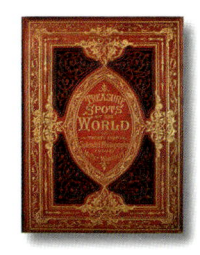

Treasure Spots of the World was unique when it appeared in 1875. Illustrated with permanent photographs, guaranteed never to fade, it used the work of nineteen photographers to create a journey for armchair tourists.

The Alcazar in Seville, photographed by John Stuart.

Newcastle, a 'somewhat dingy town' of 150,000 inhabitants, best known for its 'large ship-building yards and manufactories of locomotives and iron goods', according to Baedeker, who thought the High Level Bridge 'a triumph of engineering'.

Newcastle could be reached from London in between seven and nine hours, and the guidebook started its Newcastle city tour from the Central Station, touching on the two cathedrals, the castle and the High Level Bridge, described as 'a triumph of engineering skill, designed by Robert Stephenson, of which Newcastle is justly proud'. For somewhere to stay, Baedeker recommended the Station Hotel, the Central Exchange Hotel in Grey Street, and the Douglas or the County in Grainger Street West. For those with an aversion to licensed premises, there was the Tyne Temperance. Muirhead also suggested that, 'after prior application', the visitor should visit 'the Ordnance Works, Steel Works, and Shipbuilding Yard of Lord Armstrong at Elswick … which employs 16,000 people'.

Although there was a regular rail service between the two towns, he also suggested that 'A steamboat-trip (fare 6d) may be taken down the Tyne to Tynemouth', which 'is frequented for sea-bathing'. And despite the colour of the water, he noted that 'Tyne salmon have a great reputation for delicacy and flavour'. For those intent on staying in Tynemouth, the Grand, the Bath and the Royal hotels were the recommended watering places.

For the more adventurous, a train journey to Beal, followed by a boat trip or walk to Lindisfarne, was suggested, as was a train journey to Lucker, with a 10s boat trip to the Farne Islands. In those days, 10s was half the average weekly wage, so clearly that suggestion was directed at Baedeker's more affluent readers.

Karl Baedeker had started publishing guidebooks – in German – in 1829, but by the century's end he had covered most of the world in English, French and German.

The British publisher John Murray published his first travel guide, titled *A Handbook for Travellers on the Continent*, in 1836, and in 1861 Murray joined forces with Baedeker – now led by Karl's son Ernst – to publish an English-language guide to the Rhine. After Ernst's untimely death in Egypt at the age of only twenty-eight, his brother, Karl junior, took the helm, and Baedeker's range of English-language guides grew rapidly. Their first English guide, not surprisingly, was a guide to London and its environs, published in 1878 – by which time Thomas Cook, and other tour operators, were bringing American visitors to Britain in ever greater numbers.

This was not the first time that publishers had rushed to fill a void in the market created by Thomas Cook. Where the tourists went, guidebooks followed. Recalling his first Scottish tour, Cook, writing twenty years later, remarked that:

> On the occasion of our visit in 1846, a soirée was held in the Waterloo Rooms in Edinburgh to celebrate the event. At the soirée a long and most interesting epitome of the city history and local characteristics was given from the chair [by William Chambers], and in about three weeks following appeared *The Stranger's Visit to Edinburgh*, as one of a series of miscellaneous tracts then publishing by the celebrated firm of W. & R. Chambers. That little brochure, though costing but a penny, has been to us ever since one of the most interesting of the large family of Scottish Guide Books.

No late-Victorian tourist should have travelled without one of the first pocket phrase-books – this one promising useful phrases in fourteen languages.

Cook's 1874 *Tourist's Handbook to Holland, Belgium and the Rhine.*

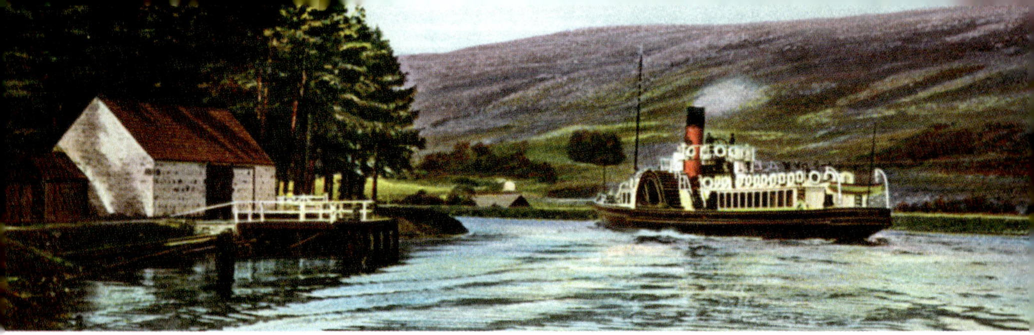

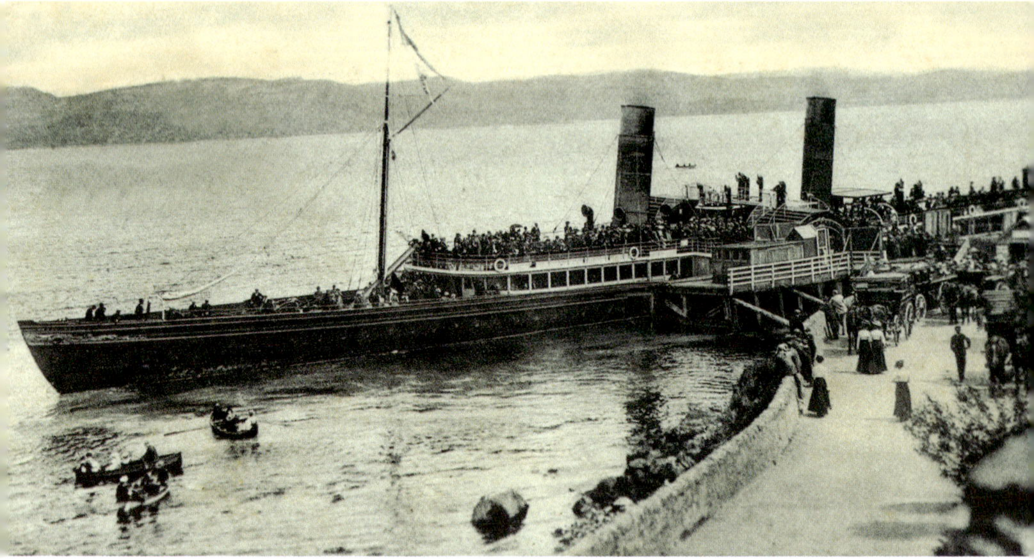

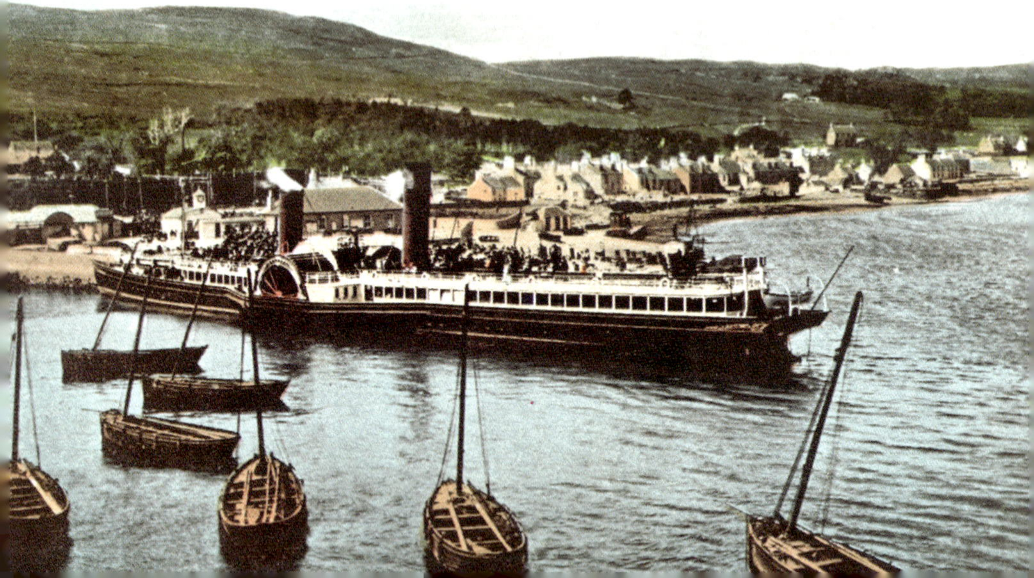

DAVID MACBRAYNE'S ROYAL ROUTES

THERE CAN BE few businessmen about whom verse has been written – and even fewer who have been the subject of rewritten psalms. On Scotland's late Victorian west coast, the usually God-fearing locals even modified the Twenty-fourth Psalm to give a sense of one man's omnipotence:

> The Earth belongs unto the Lord,
> and all that it contains.
> Except the Kyles and the Western Isles,
> for they are all MacBrayne's.

David MacBrayne operated many of the passenger steamers which sailed to the Scottish islands, and these ferries – and the people and goods they carried – were a lifeline for the remote island communities and the small ports along the shores of Scotland's western sea lochs. They were also the means by which Victorian tourists explored the area –which they did in huge numbers.

The company can trace its origins back to 1851, and, as Caledonian MacBrayne, it is still at the heart of travel off Scotland's west coast today. When it was established, the enterprise was known as David Hutcheson & Company, and MacBrayne himself was just a junior partner. His pedigree, however, was high – he was the nephew of the brothers George and James Burns, whose shipping empire was already substantial. Hutcheson was a cousin of the Burns brothers, and it was the decision of George and James to divest themselves of their local shipping interests and concentrate on transatlantic traffic which gave Hutcheson and MacBrayne the opportunities they needed. David Hutcheson & Company acquired the Scottish interests of G. & J. Burns and never looked back.

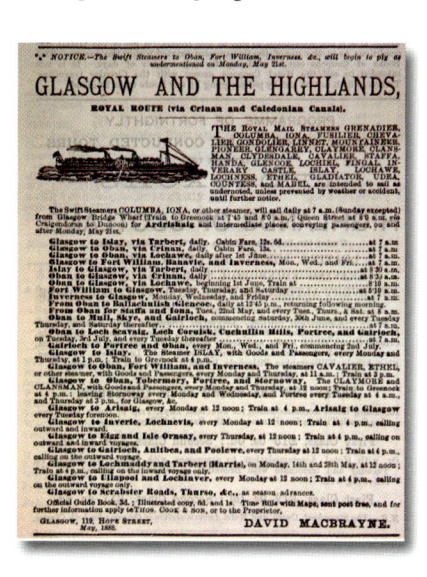

Opposite top: One of MacBrayne's steamers on the Caledonian Canal in 1908.

Opposite middle: PS *Columba*, seen here at Tarbert pier, was built for MacBrayne's in 1878 by J. & G. Thomson at Clydebank (the yard which became John Brown & Co in 1899), and served the Tarbert to Ardrishaig route for fifty-seven years.

Opposite below: Taken at Ardrishaig in the mid-1890s and published in the 1897 edition of MacBrayne's *Summer Tours in Scotland*, this view of the PS *Columba* appeared as a postcard c. 1904.

Left: MacBrayne's 'Royal Routes', as advertised in *Cook's Excursionist*.

THE VICTORIAN AND EDWARDIAN TOURIST

Opposite:
David MacBrayne commissioned the building of the SS *Linnet* in 1866 specifically for his 'Royal Route to the Isles'. She connected with steamers from Glasgow at Ardrishaig and ferried passengers the 8½ miles along the Crinan Canal to Crinan, where another steamer would be waiting to take them onwards to Oban and the Western Isles. *Linnet* worked the service for sixty-three years.

SS *Linnet* enters Cairnbaan Lock on the Crinan Canal in 1906.

Things went well for George Burns as well – he was one of the founder investors in the British & North American Royal Mail Steam Packet Company established in 1839, initially operating regular sailings from Glasgow and Liverpool to Halifax and Boston. The largest investor in that enterprise was Canadian-born Samuel Cunard, and after forty years, and a series of mergers and acquisitions, the company was renamed the Cunard Steamship Company in 1879.

Two years earlier, in 1877, David Hutcheson had retired, and his brother Alexander left the company in 1879, leaving MacBrayne as sole owner, and so, in the same year that the Cunard Steamship Company was formed, the ferry company changed its name to David MacBrayne Ltd.

Western Scottish ferry routes, in the closing years of the nineteenth century, soon became dominated by a small number of operators: the Clyde coast was dominated by railway company steamers, but MacBrayne's and the Caledonian Steam Packet Company, which had been set up in 1889 by the Caledonian Railway, effectively controlled the routes to the islands. Rivalry was intense, and the quest for success led to the construction of some of the finest paddle-steamers of the age. Companies competed to offer more frequent services, faster sailings, greater comfort, and better on-board facilities.

MacBrayne's – and Hutcheson's before them – were responsible for building some of the fastest and finest steamers, many of them bearing names which have continued to be used throughout the fleet. In 1855 they built the first steamer to carry the name *Iona* – built especially for what had become

DAVID MACBRAYNE'S ROYAL ROUTES

A 1904 postcard of Oban Bay. Oban is still the departure point for many of MacBrayne's vessels today.

Oban station, seen here in 1906, offered direct train services to and from Glasgow.

known as the 'Royal Route to the Isles'. *Iona* was sold after seven years and was used to run the blockade during the American Civil War. Her replacement of the same name was also sold to the Americans but sank off Lundy on her outward journey. The third *Iona* was launched in 1864 and served the company for over forty years.

MacBrayne's 'Royal Route' from Glasgow to Inverness via Ardrishaig, Oban and Fort William was so named because Queen Victoria had made that

DAVID MACBRAYNE'S ROYAL ROUTES

Photographers loved this view of Corpach Pier with the mountains behind. The 1888-built steamer *Fusilier* stands at the quay while a horse-drawn omnibus waits to collect passengers. *Fusilier* spent forty-six years of her fifty-year life operating the Oban to Fort William service.

Built in 1866, the PS *Gondolier*, seen here in 1903, spent seventy-three years working the Caledonian Canal between Banavie and Inverness. She was built for David Hutcheson & Co by J. & G. Thomson.

The PS *Gairlochy* on the Caledonian Canal near Fort Augustus. Bought second-hand by MacBrayne, she was nearly fifty years old when this Edwardian photograph was taken.

57

A David Hutcheson advertisement in the *North British Advertiser*, July 1853.

> REDUCTION of FARES by First-Class Return Tickets, available within Fourteen Days, by Royal Route via Crinan and Caledonian Canals.
> **GLASGOW AND THE HIGHLANDS,**
> Unless prevented by circumstances.
> The Swift Steamer MOUNTAINEER, leaves Glasgow Bridge Wharf Daily, (except Sunday,) at 7 A.M., for ARDRISHAIG, conveying Passengers only
> FOR OBAN AND FORT-WILLIAM
> daily (except Sunday) at 7 A.M.;
> FOR INVERNESS
> every Monday, Wednesday, and Friday, at 7 A.M.
> FROM OBAN TO STAFFA AND IONA
> every Tuesday, Thursday, and Saturday.
> FROM OBAN TO GLENCOE AND GLENFINNAN
> every Monday, Wednesday, and Friday.
> FROM INVERNESS TO GLASGOW,
> The EDINBURGH CASTLE every MONDAY, WEDNESDAY, and FRIDAY, at 7 A.M.
> FROM FORT-WILLIAM AND OBAN TO GLASGOW.
> From Fort-William daily (except Sunday), about 5 A.M., and from Oban about 7 A.M., arriving at Glasgow same afternoon.
> FOR LOCHCORRISKIN AND THE COOLIN HILLS,
> as the Season advances.
> FROM OBAN, TOBERMORY, PORTREE, AND STORNOWAY, calling at the various intermediate ports, the CHEVALIER every Thursday at 2 P.M., Train, 4 P.M. The CHEVALIER proceeds on 4th and 25th August, to *LOCHINVER*; on 21st July and 11th August, to *GAIRLOCH*; on the 28th July and 18th August, to *LOCHMADDY*; and on 11th August and 1st September, to *SCRABSTER, THURSO.*
> The Steamers CYGNET and LAPWING Sail for OBAN, FORT-WILLIAM, AND INVERNESS, every Friday at 2 P.M., Train 4 P.M., and on Mondays the 18th July, 1st, 15th, and 29th August, at 2 P.M., Train 4 P.M. OBAN, TOBERMORY, COLL, TIREE, AND LOCH BOISDALE, on Mondays the 25th July, 8th and 22 August, at 2 P.M., Train 4 P.M.
> Glasgow, 15th July 1853. HUTCHESON & CO., 14, Jamaica Street.

The Caledonian Steam Packet Company's steamer PS *Kylemore* – previously known as *Britannia* and then as *Vulcan* – pulls out from the Broomielaw on the Clyde past MacBrayne's 1864-built PS *Iona*, c. 1905.

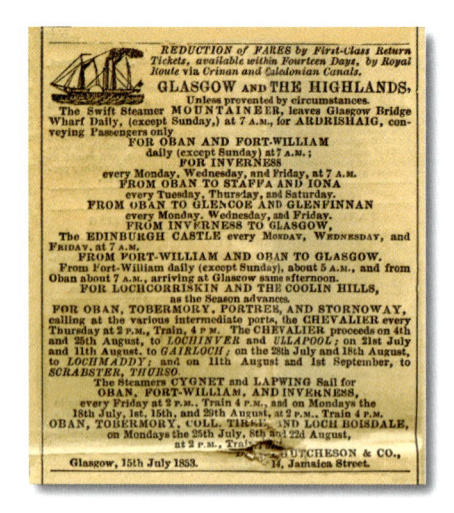

journey in 1847. On that occasion, the Queen had travelled in great style. In her *Leaves from the Journal of Our Life in the Highlands*, she wrote that she had 'entered a magnificently decorated barge, drawn by three horses, ridden by postillions in scarlet', for the journey along the Crinan Canal to Lochgilphead.

By 1897, passengers could leave Glasgow on board the 'swift steamer' PS *Cavalier* at 1 p.m. on a Monday, and disembark at Muirtown Locks at Inverness by 4 p.m. on Wednesday. The 1897 timetable promised that 'cabs and omnibuses from the different hotels await the steamer's arrival at Muirtown'. For those with the time and the money to afford such a trip, the company advertised that the overnight cabins on the vessel were equipped with electric lights. The round-trip fare, 'with first-class sleeping accommodation', cost £2, or £3 10s with all meals included.

DAVID MACBRAYNE'S ROYAL ROUTES

Many Inverness hotels advertised in A. & C. Black's 1897 *Picturesque Guides* – some including prices. Most assured visitors that they met all the Caledonian Canal steamers.

Steamers arrived at the quayside at Muirtown Locks just outside Inverness – seen here in 1904 – where coaches and omnibuses from all the rival hotels lined up at the jetty, to pick up their passengers. The number of waiting vehicles attests to the popularity of the service.

Along the way *Cavalier* – under the command of Captain D. McTavish – put in at no fewer than nineteen piers. Passengers without cabins could enjoy five-star catering in the steamer's luxurious dining saloon – if they could afford it. A breakfast fit for a king could be purchased for 2s, a four-course luncheon for 3s, and a 'high tea' for 2s.

59

From the 1890s, to help their passengers enjoy their trips, MacBrayne's produced detailed guidebooks. Their fleet of thirty-three vessels was among the finest on the west coast and the company's *Summer Tours in Scotland* books detailed the sights along the river Clyde as the steamers made their way slowly towards the estuary.

The books not only described the towns along the way, but also identified each dock, and each shipyard, detailing which of their steamers had been built at which yard. For the interested traveller, statistics were there in abundance – the population of Greenock in 1897, for example, was 70,000. Today, although the town covers a greater area, its population is around 45,000.

Well before the end of Victoria's reign, the railway companies and the steamship companies co-operated to offer 'Circular Tour' tickets. Steamers

For the 3-D enthusiast, stereoscopic views of the steamers were available. Here SS *Linnet* is passing through one of the locks on the Crinan Canal in the late 1890s.

Below:
At Prince's Pier, Greenock, railway passengers from Glasgow could meet the MacBrayne's steamers.

60

could be taken from Glasgow to Oban – travelling to Ardrishaig, passing through the Crinan Canal on board the SS *Linnet*, and then getting a third boat up the coast to Oban. The return journey was by train from Oban via Crianlarich. Three classes of fare were offered: a first-class cabin cost 1 guinea return, a second-class cabin 16s, and travelling steerage on deck cost half a guinea (10s 6d).

Leaving Broomielaw Quay in Glasgow at 7 a.m. entailed getting up at a very early hour, but it was worth it. MacBrayne's 1897 *Summer Tours* advised travellers that:

> The sail down the river will, on a fine morning, especially if it be high-water, amply repay the tourist for getting up earlier than is absolutely necessary... The steamer, however, can be overtaken at Prince's Pier, Greenock, about 9 a.m., by trains in connection with the Midland, and Glasgow and South Western Railways; at Gourock pier; about 9.15 a.m., by trains in connection with the London & North Western, and Caledonian Railways; and at Dunoon about 9.30 a.m., by trains via Craigendoran, in connection with Great Northern, North Eastern, and North British Railways.

By the early years of the twentieth century, and the arrival of the age of the postcard, ferry companies quickly realised that selling postcards of their vessels was a good way of earning publicity and promoting their routes.

Four fishing smacks make their way out of the lock at Tomnahurich on the Caledonian Canal, c.1906.

THE VICTORIAN AND EDWARDIAN TOURIST

A crofting family on Lewis, as depicted on a locally produced postcard from 1902.

The craze for collecting postcards was already in full swing by the middle of the Edwardian decade, and MacBraynes encouraged postcard publishers to photograph their vessels. Rival companies vied with each other for the most striking views, or the finest tinting. The Crinan Canal's SS *Linnet* alone was the subject of over twenty cards. Thus, a considerable number of fine views of the company's steamers have been handed down to us.

As the number of Edwardians taking MacBrayne's tours increased, both local and national postcard publishers were quick to supply them with a range

Whelk gatherers at Kerrycroy on the Isle of Bute, from a postcard mailed in 1903.

62

of views which focused on the unique character of the islands and west coast communities they were visiting. For city dwellers, the simple lifestyles of the islanders were very different from their own, and, for the islanders, posing for such postcards probably brought a little additional income.

Above: Near Stornoway on the Isle of Lewis, two girls pose for the camera in 1903 on their way home laden with peat. 'This is the style of most of the girls around the port,' said the message on the back, addressed to Miss Lloyd in Clitheroe.

Middle: A farmyard at Ettrick on the Isle of Bute, c.1903; photographed and published by Whiteford of Rothesay.

Drystone cottages on Skye: a late-Victorian photograph used as an Edwardian postcard.

Barrow Falls, Derwentwater.
G. W. Wilson.   No. 588.   Aberdeen.

EXPLORING THE ENGLISH LAKES

ONE OF THE EARLIEST AIDS to travellers in Cumbria (the area of the modern county covers what were then separate counties of Cumberland and Westmorland, and part of Lancashire) was *Sylvan's Pictorial Handbook to the English Lakes*, published in 1847. Its writer predicted the immense popularity of walking and touring holidays in the Lake District which we recognise and enjoy today, and saw the opening of the railway as the catalyst which would bring about that popularity. Hitherto, access to the Lakes from London had been a slow and inconvenient journey, either by train to Liverpool, a steamer to Ulverston and then a coach journey, or by mail coach to Lancaster. The railway link had been opened only the previous year, and its popularity had yet to be tested.

While Sylvan cannot have imagined just how popular the region would become, he did predict a huge influx of visitors to the area. He wrote in his introduction:

> When it is generally known that in about twelve hours the Tourist may be set down at Kendal, direct from London – at the very gate as it may be termed, of a district universally admitted to be the most beautiful in England – it is not too much to assert that the number of Tourists will annually increase.

Not everyone was enamoured of the increasing numbers of tourists brought by the railway – or indeed by the intrusion of the railway itself. There were some very vocal critics throughout the nineteenth century, among them such luminaries as William Wordsworth, John Ruskin, Canon Hardwicke Rawnsley, Beatrix Potter and Octavia Hill. Their concerns were not just about the railway itself – which they saw as a noisy, smelly blight on the unspoilt beauty of the Lakes – but about the increasing numbers of what they termed 'bungalow-builders' from Manchester and Liverpool who found that easier access made the area ideal for second homes. A number of those objectors eventually set up the National Trust as a means of protecting England from what they perceived as the ravages of modernity.

Sylvan's writing style was somewhat anodyne, with literal accounts rather than the more romantic descriptions of Lakeland which pepper the work of later authors. Indeed, most guidebooks from the mid-nineteenth century onwards not only waxed lyrical about the scenery, but also included guidance for their readers on how and why they should appreciate that beauty. Where

Opposite:
Top: Furness Abbey, a stereo view by G.W. Wilson of Aberdeen, 1860s.

Middle: Cartes-de-visite. Borrowdale from above the Bowder Stone, G.W. Wilson, 1860s. Unidentified Lakeland waterfall, M. Bowness, late 1850s. Barrow Falls, Derwentwater, G.W. Wilson, 1860s.

Bottom: A coach disembarks its passengers at the Kirkstone Pass Inn, from a carte-de-visite print, late 1850s.

THE VICTORIAN AND EDWARDIAN TOURIST

London Euston Station, c. 1910. The journey time of 'about twelve hours' referred to by Sylvan in his *Pictorial Handbook to the English Lakes* had been reduced to about nine by this time. Until 1909, Euston was known as Euston Square, but 'Square' was dropped from its name when Gower Street station on the Metropolitan Railway was renamed Euston Square.

The steamer *Swift*, already heavily laden, approaches Windermere Pier, c. 1903.

Visitors cruising aboard the steam yacht *Swan*, also on Windermere, c. 1906. *Swan*, launched in 1869, sailed until 1938.

Sylvan included more eloquent descriptions, they are often quotations from other writers. Windermere, he suggested, was 'as Dr Mackay says, "beautiful beyond expression, and the admiration of even the dullest of travellers"'. One has to ask, would the 'dullest of travellers' have embarked upon the twelve-hour journey from London to admire the lake in the first place?

The steamers *Swift* and *Tern* and the cargo steamer *Raven* at Lakeside Pier, Windermere, c. 1904. *Swift* (built 1900) remained in service until 1981; *Tern* (1890) still sails the lake today.

THE VICTORIAN AND EDWARDIAN TOURIST

Above: 'Yacht Race, Windermere', a Valentine postcard from c. 1905

Right: A carte-de-visite published by the Manchester Photographic Company in the 1860s. The hotel distributed these as advertising. Thomas Cook's guide for 1888 states that hotel vouchers for the Ullswater Hotel cost 11s per day for full board. Baedeker's *Guide to Great Britain* for 1890 notes that 'About 1 M. to the N., on the E. bank of the lake, near the steamboat-pier, is the large Ullswater Hotel (table d'hote 4s, R. & A. 4s), with pleasant grounds'. Dinner and room at 8s in 1890 was a significant outlay. 'R & A' stood for 'room and attendance', meaning that a servant was assigned exclusively to the room. A bedroom without attendance would have cost much less. For the additional 3s, Cook's tourists got breakfast, afternoon tea and supper. Having given quite a good account of the hotel, Baedeker did warn that 'On the hillside above the Ullswater Hotel are the *Greenside Lead Mines*, which send a stream of polluted water into the lake'.

68

Derwentwater and Skiddaw, and Lyulph's Tower, Ullswater. Two cartes-de-visite from the 1860s by Thomas Ogle of Penrith. Born in Preston, Ogle had worked as a bookbinder and a drawing teacher before taking up portrait photography c. 1855. He moved to Grange-over-Sands on the fringe of the Lake District c. 1862 and, after relocating his business to Penrith, marketed an extensive series of cartes-de-visite and tinted stereoscopic views of Lakeland scenery. For the wealthier tourist, he published several books of views, and his images were used to illustrate the book *Our English Lakes, Mountains, and Waterfalls, as seen by William Wordsworth* (1864), which used views of the Lake District – and of the poet's house at Rydal Mount – to accompany Wordsworth's poems.

If potential visitors bought his 250-page guide before embarking on the train, they could have read it from cover to cover before reaching Kendal, and still have had little feeling for the spectacular scenery they were about to experience. But visit the Lakes they did, in many thousands each year, and, despite those eminent objectors, Lakeland did its best to cater for them – and perhaps educate them a little in the appreciation of natural beauty along the way.

From the earliest days of practical photography, studios opened up in the main Lakeland towns, and a number of photographers set out to capture the beauty of the area in extensive collections of tourist views. Cartes-de-visite

69

THE VICTORIAN AND EDWARDIAN TOURIST

for the family album, large-format views to be pasted into larger albums and folios, and three-dimensional views for the drawing-room stereoscope all sold in large numbers. The names of Alfred Pettit of Keswick, Thomas Ogle of Penrith, Abrahams of Keswick, the Manchester Photographic Company, and many others, all grace some remarkable early views. Local photographers did not have it all their own way, however, with Francis Frith of Reigate and George Washington Wilson of Aberdeen also publishing many Lakeland views. In some cases they sent their own photographers to the area; in others they bought negatives taken by local studios.

Many of the early photographic studios also entered the highly lucrative postcard market in the early twentieth century, producing some beautiful scenic cards, and offering us some tantalising glimpses of Lakeland holidays a century and more ago.

For the visitors, the range of attractions was broadened as the years passed. While it was initially the rugged landscape and the joy of walking which drew people to the Cumberland hills, the ease of rail travel soon widened the area's appeal, aided by Thomas Cook, and others who followed his pioneering ideas on package holidays.

The first steamer appeared on Windermere as early as 1845 – amid protests from the landed gentry, who saw it as the first step towards the loss of the lake's serenity. The wooden *Lady of the Lake* spent twenty years sailing between Newby Bridge and Ambleside and was joined in 1846 by *Lord of the Isles*. 'Although the rapid movements of the little steamer, the *Lady of the Lake*,

The Mortal Man Inn at Troutbeck, not far from Windermere and Ambleside, has been a popular place for visitors to stay for over three hundred years. In 1907, it was the subject of this delightful postcard by Abrahams of Keswick, which included a verse about the beer sold by the landlady, Sally Burton. The inn's sign today, however, refers to 'Sally Birkett's ale' rather than Sally Burton's.

(Copy of old Sign on the Inn)
"O Mortal Man that lives by bread,
What is it makes they nose so red?
Thou silly fool that looks so pale
'Tis drinking Sally Burton's ale!
(Sally Burton was the old landlady)."

slightly disturb the quiet waters,' wrote Sylvan, 'it is only to subside again to an apparently greater calm.'

Successive boats increased in capacity as visitor numbers grew, introducing some beautiful vessels to the lake. One of the most graceful, *Tern*, launched in 1891, still sails today. Steamers were soon introduced on Ullswater; one of them, also named *Lady of the Lake*, launched in 1877, is claimed to be the oldest working passenger vessel in the world. Indeed, Thomas Cook was one of the driving forces behind the development of Ullswater cruises, specifically for the benefit of his tour customers.

The steamers provided both a tourist experience in themselves, and also a means of getting around the area, connecting with trains or coaches along the way. The Furness Railway branch line to Lakeside Pier at the foot of Windermere gave direct access to the steamers, and thus to the major tourist destinations along Windermere's eastern shore. The trains of the heritage Lakeside & Haverthwaite Railway and the boats of Windermere Cruises maintain that link to this day.

One of the great visitor attractions of the Lake District was the renowned Grasmere Sports, which drew huge crowds of both locals and visitors. Established in 1852, the event had grown out of smaller sports meetings and wrestling competitions throughout the area, tracing their roots back to the early nineteenth century. After the railway reached Windermere in 1846, annual attendances increased markedly, and crowd numbers continued to grow throughout the century.

Beneath the 'grandstand' sign, renowned wrestler George Steadman of Asby, near Appleby, takes on Hexham Clarke at the famous Grasmere Sports in 1896, photographed by Lakeland photographer Henry Mayson. Steadman retired from the sport in 1900, aged fifty-four, having won more than thirty trophies at the event, including fourteen heavyweight championships. He died in 1904.

The Eskdale Express at Boot station. The narrow-gauge railway was popular among tourists, although originally built to carry iron ore to Ravenglass. The 3-foot-gauge railway first carried passengers in 1876, but went out of business in 1908. This postcard dates from c. 1905. The track was relaid in 1916 by W. J. Bassett-Lowke at 18-inch gauge and reopened as the Ravenglass & Eskdale Railway.

From 1875, there was an attraction for those looking for something more spiritual, when the first Keswick Convention was held in a large tent in the town. The Convention, which has Bible study at its core, continues today, still drawing large attendances.

With the railways bringing tourists in increasing numbers, the Lake District infrastructure was barely able to cope, and in the second half of the nineteenth century many hotels were built to cater for the influx. In the more remote areas, long-established inns offered rudimentary accommodation, and those on the coaching routes did very well out of it.

Thomas Cook's tours brought larger and larger parties of people, so hotels able to cater for this new class of visitor were essential. These new hotels were by no means at the bottom end of the market. Travellers in the second half of the nineteenth century who eschewed the bright lights and cheap boarding houses of the seaside resorts for the tranquillity of a tour of the Lakes were, generally speaking, looking for a higher degree of sophistication in the places in which they stayed. But perhaps what they were looking for was not quite as sophisticated as Brownrigg's Patterdale Hotel, which advertised its prices in A. & C. Black's *Guide to the English Lakes* in 1866. From that guidebook we learn that it claimed to be:

The Oldest-Established Hotel in the District, and the only Hotel which has the right of Fishing on Lake Ullswater. This Hotel, which has recently received considerable additions, is fitted up with Hot, Cold, and Shower Baths, contains 10 Private Sitting-rooms, and every other accommodation required in a First-Class Establishment. There is a boat-landing within 300 yards, approached from the Hotel by an excellent gravel-walk, dry and clean in all seasons.

But such luxury came at a price. The average wage in the 1860s was around £1 per week, with professions such as teaching commanding salaries of £80 to £100 per year. The advertisement reminded potential visitors that the Patterdale Hotel had been patronised by the Queen and the Prince of Wales, and various members of the aristocracy, who presumably did not demur at the prices.

Bedrooms ranged from 1s 6d to 2s 6d per night (double that if they came with a private sitting room), and meals ranged from 1s 6d to 2s for breakfast, to 2s 6d to 3s 6d for dinner. So dinner, bed and breakfast for a week came to a minimum of £2 9s, rising to a maximum of £4 14s 6d for the best room and best sitting room – almost twice a teacher's weekly earnings before tax. But, as the advertisement promised, there was 'Fresh Trout every day'. All Baedecker said of the hotel in 1890 was that it was 'well spoken of'. Much extended, the Patterdale Hotel still welcomes visitors to Ullswater, its prices more affordable than in Victorian times.

The first Keswick Convention was held in a large tent in the town in 1875. The Convention continues today, still using a huge marquee. This postcard shows the Convention tent in 1908. There were also temporary stalls selling Bibles and other religious material. Religious publishers regularly used the Convention to promote their new publications.

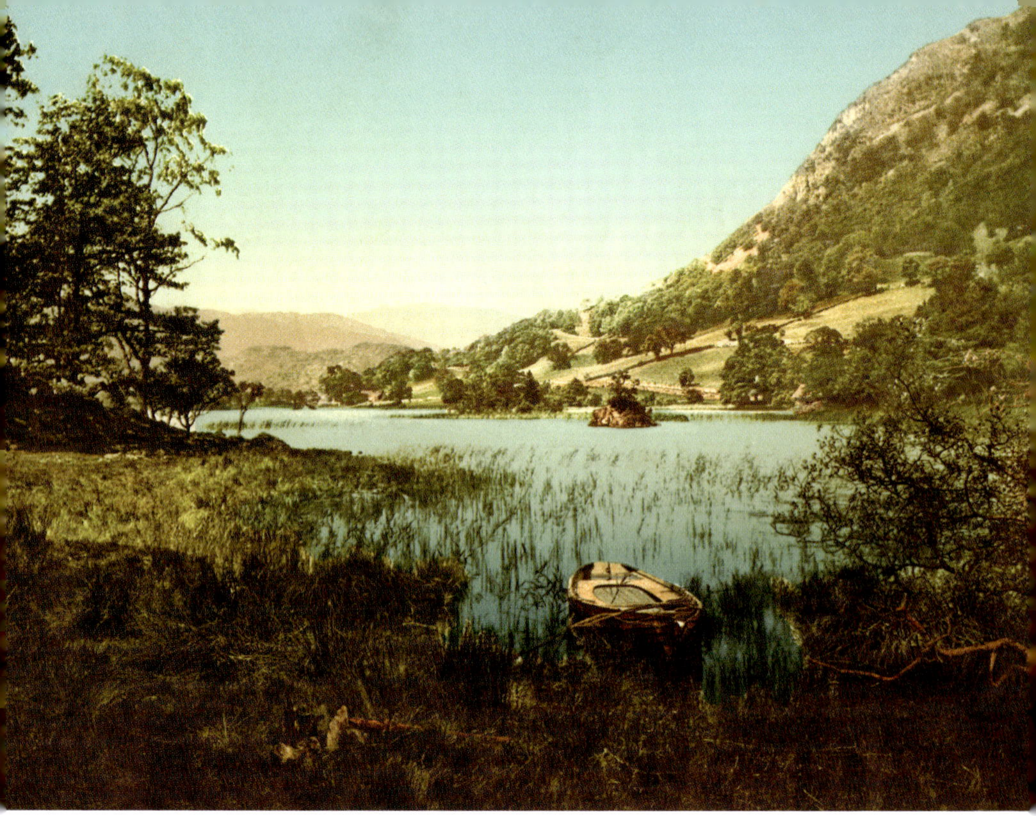

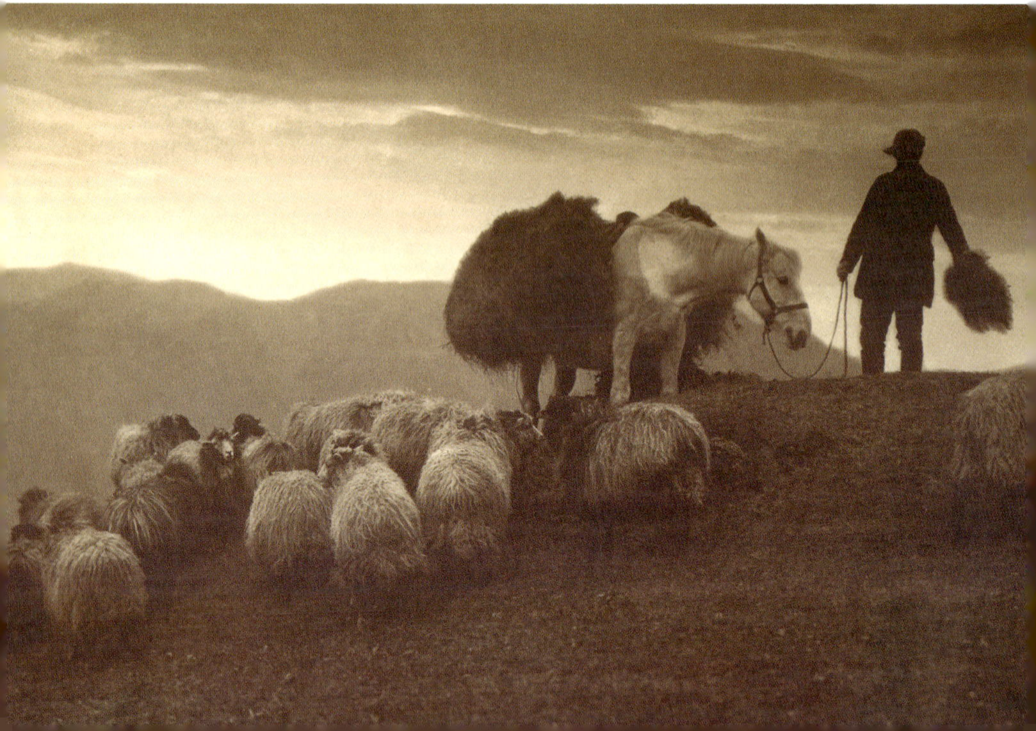

EXPLORING THE ENGLISH LAKES

Left: A multi-view postcard of Windermere from c. 1906. Cards like this were introduced for many towns and tourist areas in the late Edwardian period, and proved highly popular with visitors. The steamer illustrated is the SS *Swift*.

Bottom: Descending the Devil's Elbow on the journey back to Keswick from Buttermere. From a postcard by Abrahams of Keswick.

Baedeker reported:

> The favourite short excursion from Patterdale is that to Aira Force (4 M.), which may be made either by land or by water. In the former case we follow the pretty-wooded road along the W. bank of the lake, passing (3½ M.) the road to Troutbeck station, to the beck just beyond it. We cross the beck and ascend by the path to the left to (½ M.) the fall. To the right is Lyulph's Tower, a square ivy-clad building, the name of which, like that of the lake itself, is said to commemorate a Baron de L'Ulf of Greystoke.

A guidebook was available from a kiosk at the falls. Baedeker's writer, J. F. Muirhead, thought it quite unnecessary. With Baedeker's *Guide to Great Britain* already to hand, it probably was.

Opposite top: Rydal Water, a Photochrom print from 1898.

Opposite bottom: 'Foddering the Herdwick Hogs', one of the most popular photographs sold to tourists by the Walmesley Brothers of Keswick, 1890s.

75

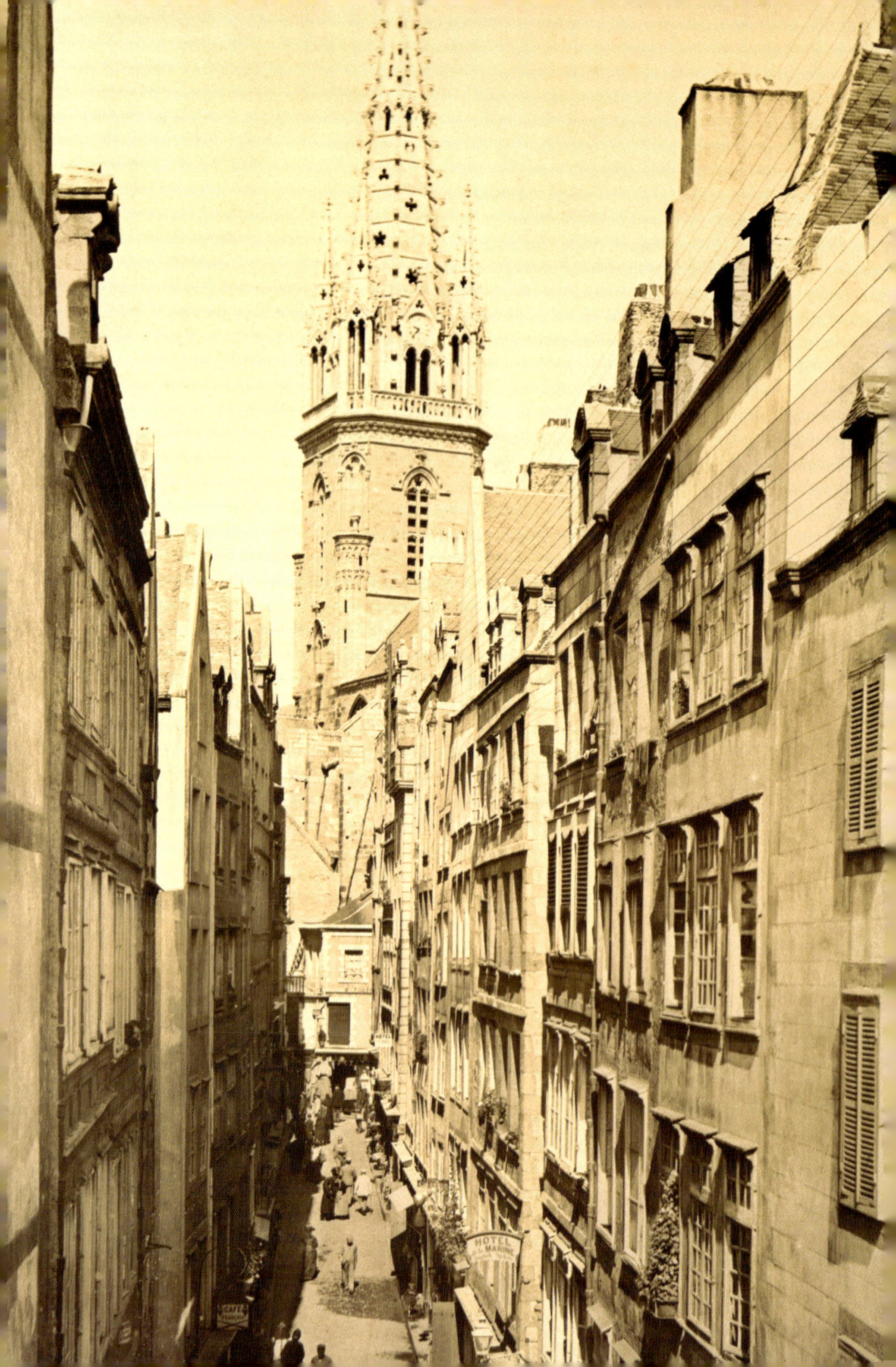
HOTEL

'ON THE CONTINONG'

EVEN IN THE EARLY YEARS of the twentieth century, continental travel was a novelty to most people – so much so that in 1908 the photographic magazine *Focus*, under the heading 'On the Continong', offered advice to travellers on what to do and not to do when visiting France. 'Rambler' writes:

> Facilities for going abroad are now so great that thousands leave our shores annually, coming back full of the sights they have seen; and I am afraid sometimes by their incessant prattle of 'when I went abroad' etc., make their friends wish they had stopped there.

The advice continued with tips on how to avoid falling out of the bunk on the steamer across the Channel, how to ease one's way through French customs – notoriously rigorous at quiet times, and how not to incur the wrath of hoteliers. 'Rambler' wrote:

> The class of people this is written for are in the habit of dining at midday, but when staying in hotels, and particularly on the Continent, where even the *artisan* has his evening dinner, it is the height of folly and extravagance to want your meals in the same way as at home.

Some of today's bad habits, it seems, have their roots at least a century ago. 'Rambler' urged:

Opposite: Despite the Reverend Thomas Raven's dismissal of the port, Saint-Malo had much to engage the tourist. This large-format tourist image from the late 1860s, by an unknown photographer, shows La Grande Rue.

Left: The west front of the cathedral at Amiens, a carte-de-visite from the late 1860s.

Below:
Notre Dame, Paris, from the south-east; carte-de-visite, mid-1860s.

Bottom: The harbour at Dinan, the port into which Thomas Raven sailed from Saint-Malo with his family in 1857.

If you are in difficulty, or want to know anything, ask the first intelligent-looking individual you see if he can speak English. If he can, your trouble is ended, but if he cannot, don't try to make him understand by shouting and using pidgin English that at home would label you a lunatic. Somehow or other an idea seems to prevail that shouting will make a foreigner understand, and how ridiculous that is, only a very little consideration will show. If you cannot make yourself understood, smile politely, raise your hat, pass on, and the odds are that the individual you next stop will understand you.

Fifty years earlier, at the beginning of a journey south through France, to spend a family holiday in the Pyrenees in 1857, the Reverend Thomas Melville Raven wrote in his diary: 'There is nothing picturesque in St Malo, I left the following afternoon, sailing up the river to Dinan.'

Today tourists tend to take photographs of anything and everything, but in the mid-nineteenth century the available processes were slow and difficult to manipulate, so photographers tended to set up their cameras only when something especially caught their eye. Surprisingly, perhaps, Saint-Malo held no such allure for the vicar. Early photographic processes required the photographer to coat his own papers and plates immediately before taking a photograph, and to develop them soon after exposure in the camera, so each picture could take up to an hour.

After returning to his home in Jersey at the end of the holiday, Raven wrote in the journal *Photographic Notes* in early 1858:

> I go upon the principle that 'fortune favours the brave,' (say nothing about it) take my rooms and work in them as I like. In one hotel my camera was seen, and when I went into my room at night, I found, by the towels and the toilet covers, unmistakable traces of there having been a worker of the same art before me.

Not wishing his wife to have to cope with chemical-stained towels, he complained and 'they were immediately changed but I was told "they were quite clean until they had been used by a monsieur Anglais".' Silver nitrate, an essential chemical, stained everything with which it came into contact.

Raven also noted that he had chosen his hotel in Dinan – the Hôtel de Bretagne – because it had a sturdy pump at the front door, and the staff were willing to cart water up to his room so he could develop his pictures.

'Les messieurs anglais' appear in another account of photography in France. Charles Kinnear, a Scottish amateur travelling with his camera in 1857, believed he was destined to become the first Briton to photograph Mont Saint-Michel on the Normandy coast. After watching his camera tripod legs, and then the coach wheels, sink slowly into the sand, Kinnear realised all was not going well

Mont Saint-Michel from the sands; photographer unknown, c. 1870. While earlier images were usually devoid of people, by the 1870s tourists preferred more animated views, and shorter exposure times made such views possible.

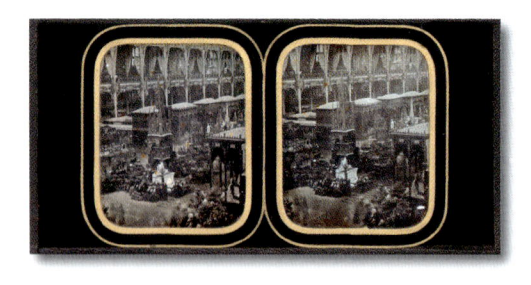

with his photography. The day was made even worse when, as he told his audience at the Photographic Society of Scotland, 'our guide assured us that it was all right, for two "messieurs anglais" had been photographing there last week'.

Until the 1890s and the advent of snapshot photography, only professional photographers and serious amateurs travelled with their cameras. The majority of the tens of thousands who travelled from Britain to France each year in the middle of the nineteenth century satisfied their wish to bring home visual memories of their travels by filling their albums with prints by local photographers, which were sold at all the major visitor attractions along their route.

As early as 1855, operators were organising package tours planned to coincide with special events. Thomas Cook was one of the pioneers, organising a continental tour which would culminate in a visit to the Exposition Universelle in Paris. His original plan to cross the Channel directly to France was thwarted when he could not negotiate a sufficiently reduced fare for his

Visitors to the 1855 Exposition Universelle could buy stereoscopic views of the interior and exterior. This daguerreotype was more expensive than a glass slide.

The *Illustrated London News* published many line illustrations of the exhibition halls, encouraging visitors to make the journey across the Channel.

'ON THE CONTINONG'

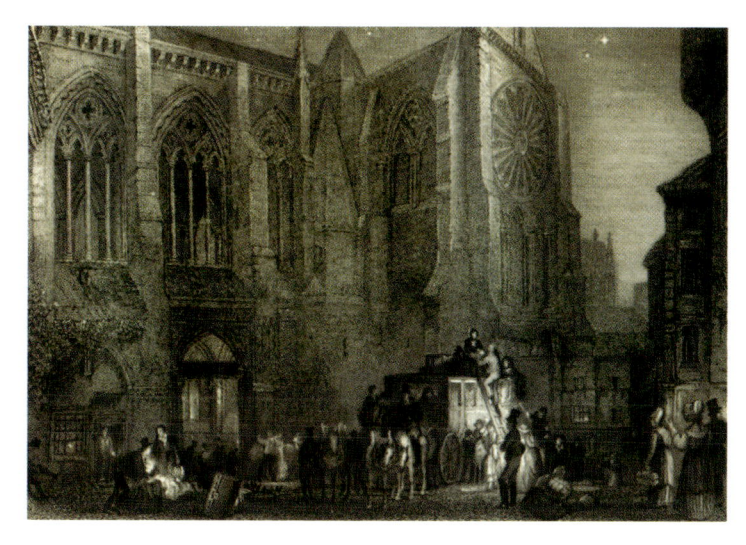

J. M. W. Turner's study of his *diligence* being loaded outside the church of St Julien at Tours, one of the engravings from *Turner's Annual Tour – Wanderings by the Loire*, 1833.

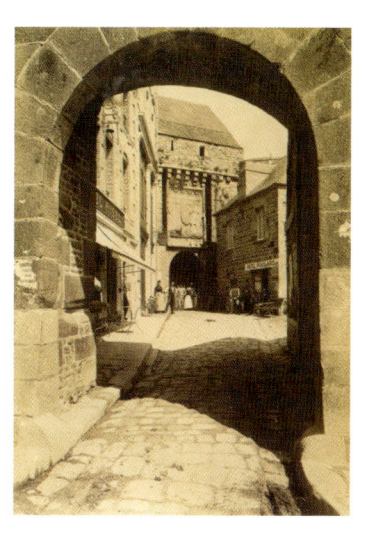

Far left: La Grande Rue, Mont Saint-Michel, 1870s; photographer unknown.

Left: La rue Jersual, Dinan, 1870s, photographer unknown, from a contemporary tourist album.

Below: A glass stereo diapositive of the Château de Chenonceau on the river Cher, photographer unknown, 1860s: a typical tourist souvenir for viewing in the drawing-room stereoscope.

fifty tourists, so they travelled to Antwerp, then Brussels, Aachen and Cologne, followed by a Rhine cruise to Mainz, before continuing to Frankfurt, Heidelberg and Strasbourg, eventually arriving in Paris.

They toured the sights of Paris before visiting the Exposition's huge Palais de l'Industrie, carrying with them cautionary

81

notes about what to do and what not to do in the city. Included in the warnings was a reminder that 'the can-can is danced by paid performers, and is altogether an unnatural and forced abandon'. It is not recorded whether that kept them away, or encouraged them to take a look.

For Thomas Cook, however, the tours he organised to France in 1855 turned in considerable losses. Other travel companies did rather better, and a substantial number of British tourists made the journey.

Touring France was popular long before Cook came on the scene, but, in the days before railways, earlier tourists were restricted in their journeys by the availability of boats and *diligences* (stagecoaches). Those were the means of travel used by the painter J. M. W. Turner for his 1826 tour of northern France and the Loire valley. The story of his journey was published seven years later as *Turner's Annual Tour – Wanderings by the Loire* with a text by Leitch Ritchie.

Turner left London for Brighton in late August, to make the Channel crossing to Dieppe. By early September he had journeyed by coach through Rouen, le Havre and Caen before staying awhile at Bayeux. From there he travelled to Isigny and on to the beautiful little Normandy port of Saint-Vaast-la-Hougue. From Saint-Vaast, he took a diligence to Barfleur and Cherbourg, arriving there on 9 September, before moving south and west to Valognes, Coutances, Granville and Avranches and on to Mont Saint-Michel, where he spent some time exploring the rock – a much quieter place then than it is today. In Turner's day the causeway did not exist, and access to the rock was either by boat or over the sands at low tide – a sometimes risky undertaking, as Charles Kinnear would discover thirty years later.

'Calaisienne' girls in traditional costume, from a postcard c. 1906.

Continuing west, Turner visited Saint-Malo, then Saint-Brieuc and Morlaix. Turning south down the Brittany coast, he arrived at Quimper on 25 September. By this time he had filled several sketchbooks with panoramas, views of buildings, and a wealth of detailed drawings of people and places, which would later form the basis for a series of paintings and engravings, which he eventually published in 1833. These sketchbooks are now in the huge collection of Turner material in the Tate.

From Quimper he headed south, arriving in Nantes, where he boarded a small boat on the Loire early in the morning on 4 October for the fourteen-hour voyage to Angers. Sketches and the

'ON THE CONTINONG'

resulting paintings from this long day's sailing confirm that the trip was completed in a single day – with sketches showing the river at Nantes at dawn, and late evening light as the boat approached Angers. Capturing the quality of the light was always of paramount importance to Turner, something to which Leitch Ritchie made reference in *Wanderings by the Loire* as he recounted his own coach ride along the riverbank:

> The water was spread out in the form of a lake, and for some time steeped in those gorgeous but delicate hues with which Turner delights to glorify his landscapes. By degree this began to fade. The glow grew colder, the light dimmer. A grey, hazy mantle unfolding itself imperceptibly, flowed from east to west. The vineyards vanished; the river rolled in vapour; tint after tint faded in the sky; the poplars themselves grew black and indefinite; and in a little while the whole world was buried in gloom.

One of Cook's accommodation cards for visitors to Paris, 1885.

With Turner's sumptuous engravings and Ritchie's evocative text, the beauty of the Loire is tangible.

By the time James and Eliza Ferguson arrived in Paris in 1874, almost everything had changed. There were fast and efficient train services, a growing number of tour companies, many more good hotels, and readily available photographic souvenirs of every memorable building and view to take back home to Britain. One thing which had not changed, however, was the power of the written word.

This was the age of letter-writing, and Eliza seems to have written home, to her mother or her brother, almost every day. To the bride from Govan, Paris and its great hotels made mixed impressions. She thought the hotel on

The harbour at Boulogne-sur-Mer, late 1860s. For many tourists arriving from Britain, this was their first view of France.

83

THE VICTORIAN AND EDWARDIAN TOURIST

Top: Dover harbour came into its own in the age of the railways. Until the end of the nineteenth century, most cross-Channel ferries were paddle-steamers, and few exceeded 1,000 tons. This is the South Eastern Railway's 996-ton *Duchess of York*, introduced on the Calais service in 1896.

Middle: 'Départ du bateau du Havre, Trouville', a postcard of c.1905.

Bottom: Boulogne-sur-Mer, c.1910. Crowds make their way from the steamer to the awaiting train in the Gare Maritime.

their first night was magnificent, but she wrote of the desk clerk:

> You have no idea how terrified both James and I were by the young man in the Grand Hotel, who had charge of the letters, and who looked so fiercely at us when we modestly gave our name, and enquired if there were any for us.

She was probably not sorry to be moved to another hotel for their second and third nights in the city, but did not mention in her letters which hotel they were moved to. Cook regularly used four Paris hotels at the time – the Grand Hotel and the Hôtel Londres et New York, both in the Place du Havre, the Saint Petersbourg at 35 Rue Caumartin, and the Hôtel Londres at 8 Rue Saint-Hyacinthe. The cosmopolitan habits of Paris failed to impress Eliza, who came from a strict Scottish Presbyterian upbringing: 'There seems to be no Sabbath-keeping here, everything going on just as on other days. It is a dreadful city!', she wrote to her brother.

It is, perhaps, easy to overlook just what an adventure crossing the Channel was in Victorian times. With today's huge cross-Channel ferries offering an uneventful passage most of the time, their 30–40,000 tons cutting smoothly through all but the stormiest of waters, our Victorian predecessors made the crossing in vessels of between 300 and 800 tons. Indeed, the South Eastern Railway's 817-ton *Mary Beatrice*, on which Mary Garnett sailed from Folkestone to Boulogne in January 1890, was considered quite a large ferry for the short crossing. She wrote in her diary:

> The *Mary Beatrice* lay waiting to receive us, and we hastened on board to dispose ourselves for a short and peaceful passage. But Biscay Bay or stormy Mediterranean never accomplished for me what this bit of choppy sea did, and Father was struck with dismay on beholding the writer reduced to all the ignomony of mal-de-mer!

The previous year, the Garnetts had sailed from Liverpool to Alexandria on board the Pappayanni Line's massive 2,445-ton paddle-steamer *Plantain*, and enjoyed a smooth passage most of the way. They had clearly expected their 1890 journey, by cross-Channel ferry and then train across France to Genoa, to be even less eventful.

Her letters, however, paint a much more vivid picture of their first visit to the south of France than her husband Robert's sketches.

A line of Brillié-Schneider motor-buses stands outside the Gare de l'Est in Paris, 1910. Paris had been operating fleets of Brillié-Schneider buses for several years by the time this postcard was published, but the longer-wheelbase vehicles seen here had been introduced only in the previous year.

Many of the gardens are fringed with hedges of juniper or cypress trees which have that peculiar soft mezzotint-like effect, they stand like tall mutes at a funeral and contrast finely with the lighter shades of colour or the metallic blue of the olives. The glowing earth lies in the narrow strata in ready prepared terraces for the husbandman to plant without the toil of digging or delving. As in every other mountainous country, here, also, the peakiest crag is tipped with tower or fortress; adding, without detraction another feature to the panorama which, as it unfolds new charms at every turn, is enshrouded in a Turneresque mist of golden light, and indeed, was it not such scenes and atmospheres that his genius has immortalized on canvas? We are now within twelve miles of Cannes and the ranges of the Estrelles are beginning to show their spurs. The shades of night are falling among camphor, tea and pepper trees.

It would be a long time before photography would be able to capture and express those elusive qualities of changing light and shade.

A decade later, the postcard era redefined the manner in which tourists communicated with those left behind at home. Now, the written description yielded to the photographic one. Perhaps more importantly, the messages on postcards quickly became more anodyne – a cursory shorthand, a message no more than a 'Wish you were here' gesture. The excursionist's personal view and account of the holiday experience were replaced by the photographer's.

Paris c. 1909, from a postcard captioned 'One of Sebrée's "Seeing Paris" sightseeing automobiles leaving the American Express Co.'s Office, 11, Rue Scribe'. Posted from Paris, 25 September 1910.

'ON THE CONTINONG'

The Hôtel de Ville, Paris, from a Louis Levy postcard, c. 1908.

Sometimes that postcard view still contained a personal resonance. 'This is the car we went on today to Menton by the Grande Corniche and La Turbie, and returned via Monte Carlo and Beaulieu,' wrote John in 1910 on a postcard to Mrs Maurice Missini, who lived at Rutland Gate in south-west London, adding that 'I am quite taken with Monte Carlo, and thinking of going to stay there tomorrow, and then go to Cannes and Grasse by the same car'. Was John, perhaps, one of those seated in the charabanc? Or had the enterprising owner simply arranged for a postcard to be available for sale to all his customers?

The postcard era ran in parallel with the growth of amateur photography, so carefully written Victorian letters were gradually replaced by increasingly ubiquitous Edwardian holiday snaps.

Like many early motor vehicles across Europe, the charabanc on which John travelled to Menton was right-hand drive.

87

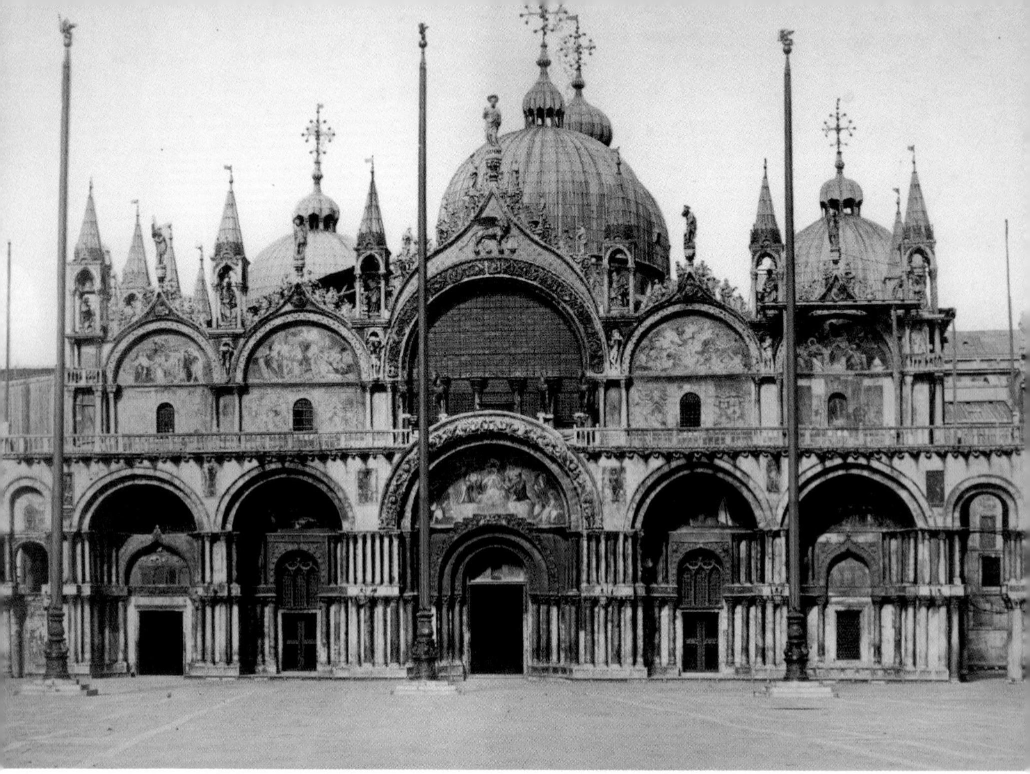

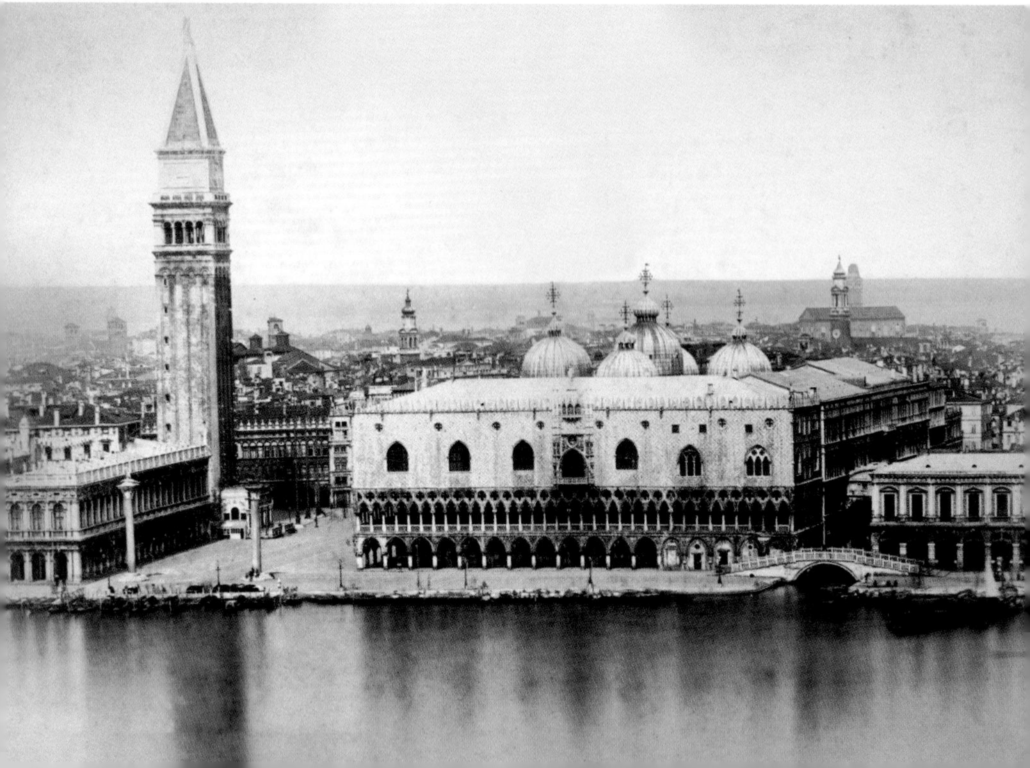

MEMENTOES OF AN ITALIAN TOUR

CARLO PONTI was a nineteenth-century romantic who both marvelled at and loved Venice. He became a master craftsman at a time when photography was challenging, slow and cumbersome. His reputation was widespread, and his photographs defined the memories brought home by tourists visiting Venice. For Ponti, with his studio door opening on to St Mark's Square, taking photographs of the Basilica San Marco presented few problems, but when working with the wet collodion process elsewhere in the city he had to take a portable darkroom with him wherever he went – for he was working at a time when photographers had to coat their own plates. An optician by training, Ponti moved to Venice in 1852, before his thirtieth birthday, and opened a shop selling optical instruments at No. 52 in St Mark's Square. By 1854, he was being awarded prizes at trade fairs in Venice for lenses he was manufacturing, and which, by that time, he was also using for his own photography. By 1855, photography was the driving influence in his life, and over the next twenty years his catalogue of views of Venice – and his sales to the burgeoning tourist trade – grew annually. A knowledge of architecture, a keen sense of history, and an eye for a great photograph were all brought together in his work.

The Venice seen in Ponti's photographs is very different in character, if not in architecture, to the city we can visit today. Because of the long exposure times needed for large-format photography in the 1850s and 1860s,

Opposite top: The main façade of the Chiesa San Marco, Venice, photographed by Carlo Ponti in the mid-1860s.

Opposite bottom: Panorama of Venice taken from the island of St George by Carlo Naya, 1860s.

Left: A carte-de-visite from the late 1860s by Carlo Ponti, showing the Natural History Museum by the side of the Grand Canal in Venice. As the museum faces north, Ponti must have taken this photograph early in the morning. When seen by most tourists, this face is in shadow.

THE VICTORIAN AND EDWARDIAN TOURIST

MEMENTOES OF AN ITALIAN TOUR

Opposite, top: The interior of the Coliseum.

Opposite, bottom: The Arch of Constantine, with the photographer's portable wet-plate darkroom on wheels set up underneath the right-hand arch.

Left: The Arch of Titus Vespasian Augustus at the entrance to the Palatine, with a lone figure – perhaps the photographer himself or his assistant – included to add scale to the scene.

most pictures from that period are devoid of people and so exude tranquillity. If someone walked across the scene during the exposure, he might appear as no more than a faint blur on the picture. To become part of the composition, he would have to stand still for quite some time. Because of the long exposure times, however, most photographers chose to take their pictures when the

The Pantheon, taken with an exposure time just short enough to record a few of the people in the square.

91

city was quiet, thus permitting them to be in total control, but giving their images the unfortunate appearance of what one critic described as 'cities of the dead'.

Ponti's business had been open only a few years when a potential rival in the tourist market, Carlo Naya, opened his studio just a few doors away, at Nos. 77–78 St Mark's Square, in 1857. Naya's standards were just as high as Ponti's, his images were available in the same range of sizes, and the quality of his work was just as appealing. Perhaps that is what eventually brought them together: with Ponti already a successful publisher of Venetian views, Naya chose not always to compete with him, but to give him marketing rights over some of his work in return for a percentage.

Both were key figures in the recording of nineteenth-century Venice, and in establishing and marketing the tourist image of the city. Their names can be found on large mounted prints, and on the small card-mounted carte-de-visite prints which fitted into the pages of the Victorian family album. Irrespective of size, they all have one thing in common: by virtue of the technology of their day, theirs is a Venice which rarely awakens, deserted both by its population and by tourists.

But long before professional photography defined the tourist image of Italy, gentlemen amateurs had been photographing the great sights as part of their Grand Tours. Among them, the Reverend Calvert Richard Jones travelled with his wife and friends on a photographic tour to Malta and Italy in the closing weeks of 1845, carrying with them a stock of calotype paper negatives prepared in advance by Henry Fox Talbot's staff at Talbot's printing works in Reading. Jones had accompanied Talbot on a photographic tour in Yorkshire earlier in the year, and Talbot had been very impressed by Jones's enthusiasm for the calotype process. Travelling abroad with his camera was the logical extension of a lifetime's enthusiasm for travel on the part of Jones and his companions. He and Kit Talbot, a cousin of the calotype inventor, had made their first Mediterranean tour in 1824, buying works of art for Kit Talbot's house, Margam Castle, in South Wales.

He had attempted to undertake a photographic tour of Italy in 1841, in the earliest months of photography. Having acquired all the paraphernalia necessary to take photographs using the French daguerreotype process, he and his wife Anne had travelled south, but his plans to 'photographize' were thwarted when the Italian customs authorities confiscated his equipment and chemicals at the port of Genoa. He eventually got his equipment back, but ran out of time before he could 'photographize' Venice. None of his early daguerreotypes is known to have survived.

Calvert and Anne Jones, Kit Talbot and his wife Charlotte, whose health the Mediterranean journey had been intended to benefit, left Britain in November 1845 for Malta, but by early April 1846 Charlotte had died, and

MEMENTOES OF AN ITALIAN TOUR

Pompeii was an essential stopping place on the route of the Grand Tour, and visitors have been touring the site since its rediscovery in the seventeenth century. Italian photographers made the first images of the partially excavated ruins in the early years of photography, and several British amateur photographers, including the Reverend Calvert Jones, took calotype photographs of the ruins as early as November 1845. These views, by an unknown photographer in the 1880s, show the Teatro Comico, the Tempilo di Ercole and Foro Triangolare, and the Tempilo di Isis. Images like these were sold on site for a very low price, often in sets of ten or more. The examples here are from a set depicting twenty different views of the site.

The Via and Fontana dell'Abbondanza at Pompeii; photographer unknown, 1880s.

The Ponte Vecchio in Florence, from a calotype made by Calvert Richard Jones in early 1846.

Jones and his wife continued to Italy alone, arriving in Naples in the last week of April. In the antiquities of Pompeii and of Rome, Jones found huge scope for his camera.

We know, from Talbot's instructions to him, that many of his negatives required exposure times of ten minutes or so: preparing the calotype papers back in Reading and transporting them to Malta and Italy reduced their

MEMENTOES OF AN ITALIAN TOUR

sensitivity considerably. Jones was also an accomplished artist, and many of his photographs were subsequently either overpainted with watercolours, or used as reference for a series of sketches and paintings.

Left: The Temple of Vesta and Rienzi's House, Rome, by Calvert Richard Jones, May 1846.

Below: General view of Genoa, 1870s, photographer unknown. Genoa, a brief stopover on the Grand Tour on the way from France to ancient Italy, was where Calvert Richard Jones had his daguerreotype equipment confiscated in 1841. 'Genova la Superba', wrote Mary Garnett in her diary forty years later; 'We drive first to the Italian Church of the Annunziata. Golden pillars above, Death's heads and cross bones below on the patrician tombs – for the poor folk were buried at sea "mong de fisses", says our guide, before they had a cemetery.'

THE VICTORIAN AND EDWARDIAN TOURIST

Right: In the 1860s and 1870s the carte-de-visite was the most popular tourist memento, fitting family albums worldwide. These examples show a dramatic view of the Leaning Tower of Pisa, 1860s, and the Piazza del Campo, Siena, late 1860s; both photographers unknown.

Below: Vast crowds of pilgrims and tourists gather for an Easter Sunday Papal Mass in St Peter's Square, Rome, c. 1875.

MEMENTOES OF AN ITALIAN TOUR

Top: The Forum, Rome, photographer unknown: a 10x8 inch albumen print from a late-1860s tourist album.

Above: A carte-de-visite of Verona by Giorgio Sommer, one of Italy's leading photographers, late 1860s.

Left: The interior of the Duomo, Pisa, 1860s, photographer unknown.

97

Photographs of paintings were keenly collected by tourists in the 1860s and 1870s. These four cartes-de-visite are by the Fratelli Alinari, whose photographers travelled to galleries all over Europe.

Clockwise, from top left: *Judith* by Alessandro di Cristofano di Lorenzo del Bronzino Allori. Several versions of this painting survive from the early seventeenth century. This carte-de-visite by Alinari was copied from the canvas in the Galleria Palatina in Florence.

Cleopatra by Guido Reni, in Florence's Pitti Museum. Reni painted Cleopatra four times, and she is seen here putting the asp to her breast.

Raphael's *Madonna del Belvedere*, then part of the Imperial Collection in the Belvedere, Vienna.

Maddelena by Titian, in the Museo Nazionale di Capodimonte in Naples.

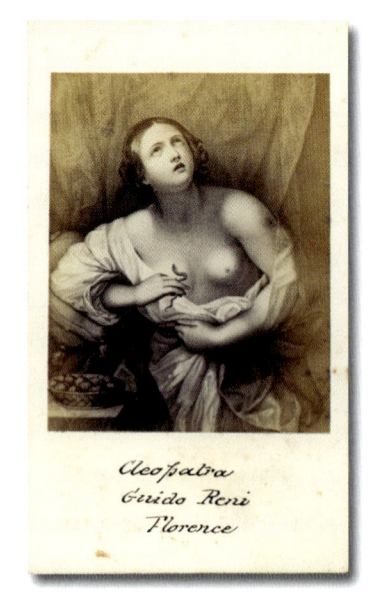

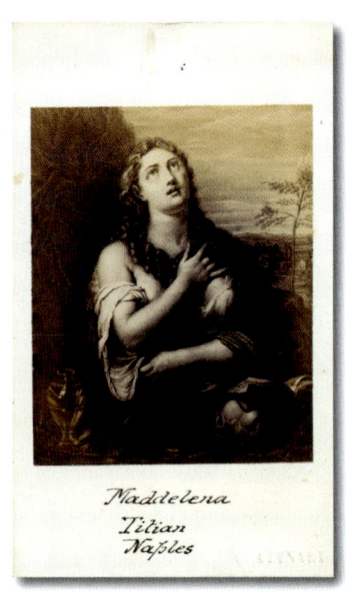

Italian professional photographers generally did not start to establish their catalogues of tourist images until the advent of the glass-plate negative, which made the mass-production of prints much quicker than was ever possible with paper negatives. The first shops selling photographs specifically taken for the burgeoning tourist trade were not established until the 1850s.

However, the new professionals went much further than simply photographing the sites of antiquity, which abounded throughout the country. They also catered for much broader tastes. By the 1860s, a wide selection of views of all the major sites along the Grand Tour was available – in every format from carte-de-visite to large 16x12 inch prints – and the popularity of such tours had a huge impact on the livelihoods of photographers throughout Europe.

But the discerning tourist expected more than just views. Albums dating from the 1860s and 1870s, while containing images of the Leaning Tower, Siena's Duomo, the major sites of Venice, and many of the historic buildings of Florence, also contain countless copies of the paintings the tourists would have seen in the great galleries of Florence, Siena and Rome. To the Victorians, sepia copies of paintings – however odd they may seem to us today – were popular. Demand was considerable, and hundreds of paintings were photographed and marketed in a variety of sizes.

That demand led to photography's first real specialists, and foremost among those in the fine-art market were the Fratelli Alinari studio in Florence's Via Nazionale, Goupil & Co of Paris, Pescio & de Carré of Genoa, and the German photographer Adolphe Braun.

While Braun concentrated mainly on large-format copies of paintings, the Alinaris and others additionally cashed in on the

Photographers were keen to let the tourists know how many awards they had won for their work. This is the back of one of Giorgio Sommer's cartes-de-visite, late 1860s.

The Castel Sant'Angelo and the River Tiber, Rome, late 1860s. To get the figures all as sharply defined as this, the unknown photographer must have persuaded them not to move during the one or two seconds exposure, and the boats must have been firmly tethered in the moving river.

growing tourist trade to produce affordable mementoes in the carte-de-visite format. By the 1870s, hundreds, if not thousands, of paintings had been photographed and marketed as cartes.

Although tourists loved them, purists hated them. Some critics saw photography as sounding the death knell of the jobbing painters who made countless copies of old masters, while others rightly lamented the fact that – as Luigi Travalloni observed – the results were, at best, the 'poorly disguised approximations of a painting which are so often the result of photographic translations'. Despite criticisms of their work, which was ground-breaking

This view of a man selling pigeon food in front of San Marco and the Doge's Palace in Venice was produced for the tourist market in 1898 using chromolithography by the Photochrom Company of Zürich. Their extensive catalogue of tourist views covered most of Europe.

in its day, Alinari photographers travelled Europe, amassing a catalogue of copies of most of Europe's great paintings.

In establishing the market for such cartes, photographers sought to set up exclusive deals with galleries for the rights to sell photographic copies, and thus were born the first photographic franchises.

By the late 1880s, visiting Italy had become much easier, with numerous companies offering to organise bespoke tours – booking tickets and hotels in advance, but leaving their tourists free to explore at their own pace. Baedeker's *Guide to Central Italy and Rome*, first published in 1867 and already in its tenth edition by 1890, was essential for the independent tourist, offering advice on almost everything the visitor needed to know.

For a more anecdotal account of Rome, one tourist noted in her diary that she had also brought Mark Twain's *The Innocents Abroad*, which she then liberally quoted from on those occasions when she thought Twain's accounts of the sights and sounds of the city were more illuminating than Baedeker's.

Doing the Grand Tour did not always leave the expected memories, as Twain enjoyed pointing out:

The Palazzo donn' Anna at Posillipo, Naples, a tinted postcard published c. 1903, and mailed on Easter Monday 1904. Local folklore associates the Palazzo by the water's edge, formerly known as La Villa Sirena, with murders, orgies and other lurid events.

At every hotel we stop at, we always have to send out for soap, at the last moment, while we are grooming ourselves for dinner, and they put it in the bill, along with the candles and other nonsense.

The experience of the Grand Tour was, sometimes, more about being seen to be 'doing the Tour' than enjoying either the travel itself or the cultural experience. And the same went for the mandatory visits to galleries. Twain wrote:

I am willing to believe that the eye of the practised artist can rest upon *The Last Supper* and renew a lustre where only a hint of it is left, supply a tint

A group of women and children pose for the photographer in a narrow alleyway in San Remo. The picture was published as a tinted postcard in 1906. San Remo had started to develop as a tourist destination in the late eighteenth century, and in the nineteenth century its position on the main railway line from Nice to Genoa helped its tourist industry thrive. Its fine hotels were favourite retreats for European royalty.

For 3-D enthusiasts, the stereoscopic view – a popular tourist memento since the 1850s – had evolved from pairs of photographic prints individually pasted on to the card, and was, by the late 1890s, being mass-produced using colour gravure printing.

that has faded away, restore an expression that is gone; patch, and colour, and add, to the dull canvas until at last its figures shall stand before him aglow with the life, the feeling, the freshness, yea, with all the noble beauty that was theirs when first they came from the hand of the master. But I cannot work the miracle. After reading so much about it, I am satisfied that *The Last Supper* was a very miracle of art once. But it was three hundred years ago.

Without doubt, had they had the courage to express themselves, many of those tourists who have stood before the painting might have agreed with him.

He also recalled a woman, on the journey back to the United States, asking her daughter 'Have we ever been to Rome?', and getting the unexpected reply 'Yes, Mother, that's where we bought those bad silk stockings.'

The Garnetts' few days in Rome were not enough, and were too quickly at an end. As they waited for the train south, Mary wrote in her diary:

Mary Garnett's diaries, and her husband Robert's sketches of their travels through Europe, Egypt and the Holy Land, were privately published in 1904.

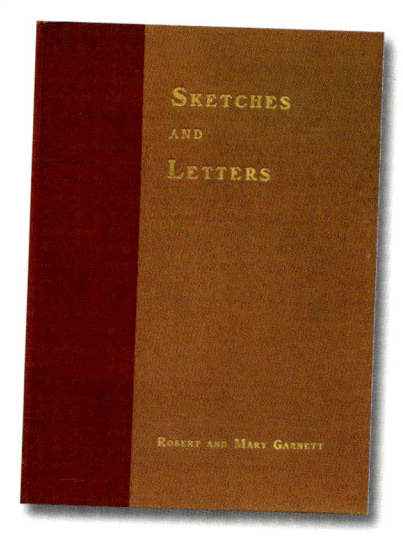

> January 29th 1890 – Whether we ever *return* or not, we leave Rome at 7.50 for Naples, feeling that we have got a very fair cursory view of it, and just gained an idea of what might be seen working away daily for a winter.

They had 'done' Rome in just five days.

More than a dozen years after returning to Warrington, and in memory of her husband who had died in the interim, Mary published her diaries, and Robert's sketches, leaving us a permanent record of their Grand Tours in 1889 and 1890.

Cook's Nile Service

P.S. "MOHAMMED ALI"

Cook's Nile Service

P.S. "MOHAMMED ALI"

OLGA

TAKING THE GRAND TOUR OF EGYPT

MARY GARNETT'S tour continued to Egypt, where the civilisation she had enjoyed in France and Italy was left far behind. When her tour party had reached the refuge of a hotel where English was spoken and writing paper was available, she wrote in her diary that:

> We have been such vagabonds upon the face of the earth, sleeping in such a variety of hotels (and such wretched berths on the *Chuzan*), and having been addressed in so many different languages, that now we really seem to have found a resting place and a home.

This was the Garnetts' second visit to Egypt, and this time their tour included a Nile cruise aboard one of the latest paddle-steamers, the *Tewfikieh*, which she described as 'one of the Kedive Line, such a pretty thing. It is quite a new company. Made their first trip last month. They have spared nothing to make their boats the perfection of comfort and good taste.' By this time – spring 1890 – several shipping companies had entered the market for Nile cruises, competing with the near-monopoly which had long been enjoyed by the Thomas Cook boats.

An interesting aspect of albums compiled by Victorian travellers undertaking the Grand Tour is the diversity of their chosen images. The photographs they brought home fall clearly into distinct groups.

The first group is the 'glory of ruins' approach to photography – images which serve the same purpose as today's picture postcards. They are the pictures which do little more than show what the places looked like. So there were images of the Sphinx – complete with an Arab sitting on top, and of the Nile with typical houses and boats. In the album from which the photographs on these pages come, all the temples and tombs are faithfully recorded, using the work of some of the finest photographers of the period. The sort of housing lived in by the indigenous population was obviously of interest to tourists, although it is clear from Mary Garnett's diary that she wished to do no more than observe it from a distance.

The second group of photographs comprises studio portraits of Arab life and costume. In a world where global communications were still almost a century in the future, what another race looked like was fascinating in itself. Before embarking on the Grand Tour, few of these wealthy travellers would ever have seen an Arab.

Opposite top:
The market at Luxor, mid-1870s, photographed by Antonio Beato, who was clearly catering for a tourist market.

Opposite inset:
The front and back of an elaborately printed passenger list for one of Thomas Cook's 1892 Nile cruises. These little cards were given to passengers to let them know who their travelling companions were.

Opposite bottom:
A cross-sail dahabiyah, 1870s, taken by the Brothers Zangaki.

The third group contains much more candid photographs: scenes of Arab life which, although posed to take account of the cumbersome photographic processes of the day, were designed to look natural. The street cafés and the street markets are little changed today.

Together, these early photographs must have been a considerable talking point when the lucky travellers returned home. The albums of images were permanent proof of the journey of a lifetime – and enduring evidence of the status of those who had been to a country which, not many years earlier, had been completely unknown to almost everyone in Britain.

Doing the Grand Tour of Egypt was as much a statement of wealth and status as it was a holiday. To have the money to afford such a trip, and to have sufficient time in which to undertake it, those who took such expeditions were necessarily from the upper classes or nouveau riche merchants.

By the late 1880s, excluding the considerable cost of getting to Cairo, a three-week Nile tour – including travel, hotels and all meals, and the assistance of dragomans when climbing the pyramids – cost around £50. With the cost of the steamer to Egypt, doing the Grand Tour cost more than the average annual wage in Britain. That cost remained unchanged for thirty years. But irrespective of how they came by their wealth, travellers arriving in Cairo were overwhelmed by the experience.

Mary Garnett, in her account of her two Grand Tours (in 1889 and 1894), which she published in 1905 after her husband's death, wrote:

EGYPTA! Our whole being thrills at the sound – it is mystery more than

Top: A meal voucher for the Nile mail-steamer service, c. 1900.

Middle: Cook's programme guide for their 1891–2 cruises on the Nile. A book such as this was published annually, giving dates, sailing times, and other essential tourist information.

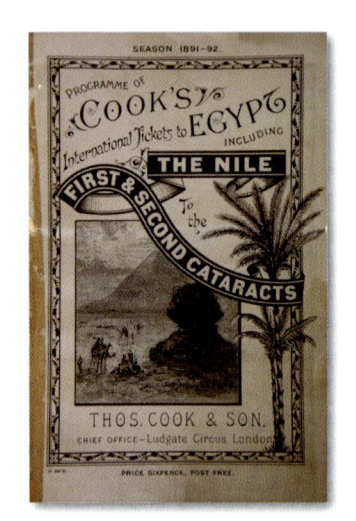

Bottom: Every passenger was given a list of the names of their fellow travellers.

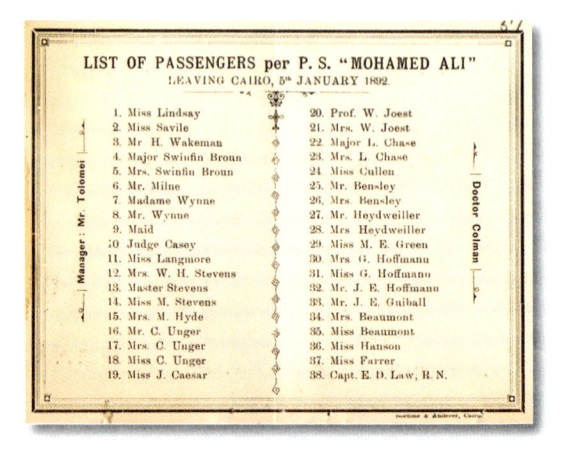

TAKING THE GRAND TOUR OF EGYPT

Antonio Beato's view of shadoofs being used to raise water from wells for irrigation. Images which showed 'real' Egyptian life were hugely popular with tourists, although actually experiencing Egyptian culture and life was to be avoided.

A Nile steamer ticket from 1893, signed by Frank Cook, Thomas's grandson.

Climbing the Pyramid of Khufu (then known as the Pyramid of Cheops) was an established part of the Victorian Grand Tour. For upper- and middle-class English ladies, holding the hands of the Egyptian dragomans who assisted their ascent was considered by some to be an act of considerable bravery. The stiff-collared husbands of some tourists felt the attention of the dragomans was an affront to their wives' modesty.

107

THE VICTORIAN AND EDWARDIAN TOURIST

Local Egyptian photographers broadened the tourists' choice of images, with views of local lifestyles. Outdoor cafés with seating, like this one, can still be found in small villages in the Nile valley today.

The gateway to the partially excavated temple at Luxor, by Antonio Beato, 1870s.

history. More strange than fiction and yet how real, for there we come to the very cradle of the human race, the germ of all civilisations, the alphabet of all science and of all art, and genesis of the earth. There is no past beyond Egypt. Let us sit down reverently before it and take a long breath. We cannot rush through such a theme. Like the patient Arab, let us take our time and leave the whirl of the Western World to its own insane speed. It will need all its hurry to catch up with us, for we are away in the dynasties and among the obelisks and sphinxes, the temples and pyramids which they may strive to copy and succeed in stealing, but can never reproduce!

Photographers did try to reproduce something of the culture and customs of the Nile valley for the tourists to take home with them, and many of them went to significant lengths to do so. The Brothers ('*Adelphoi*') Zangaki were early entrants into the market for Egyptian views, and their catalogue of photographs mirrored the itinerary of the Grand Tour. The earliest known photographs by them date from the late 1870s, and they continued to publish images of Egypt well into the postcard era. They offered views of every temple, pyramid and ancient site along the Nile from Cairo to Abu Simbel, and travelled the length of the river with a horse-drawn darkroom carrying the legend 'Zangaki Brothers' on the side.

Over the centuries, the Sphinx had become almost completely buried by the shifting desert sands, and by the early nineteenth century only the head and shoulders were visible. Work to excavate the four-thousand-year-old sculpture had started in 1817, but by the 1880s it was still only partially exposed. Excavation was not completed until the 1930s. The Arab sitting on the Sphinx's head served as a useful aid to scale, and a talking point for the tourists when they shared their memories with friends back home.

Dahabiyahs tied up at the waterfront at Luxor; photographer unknown, 1870s.

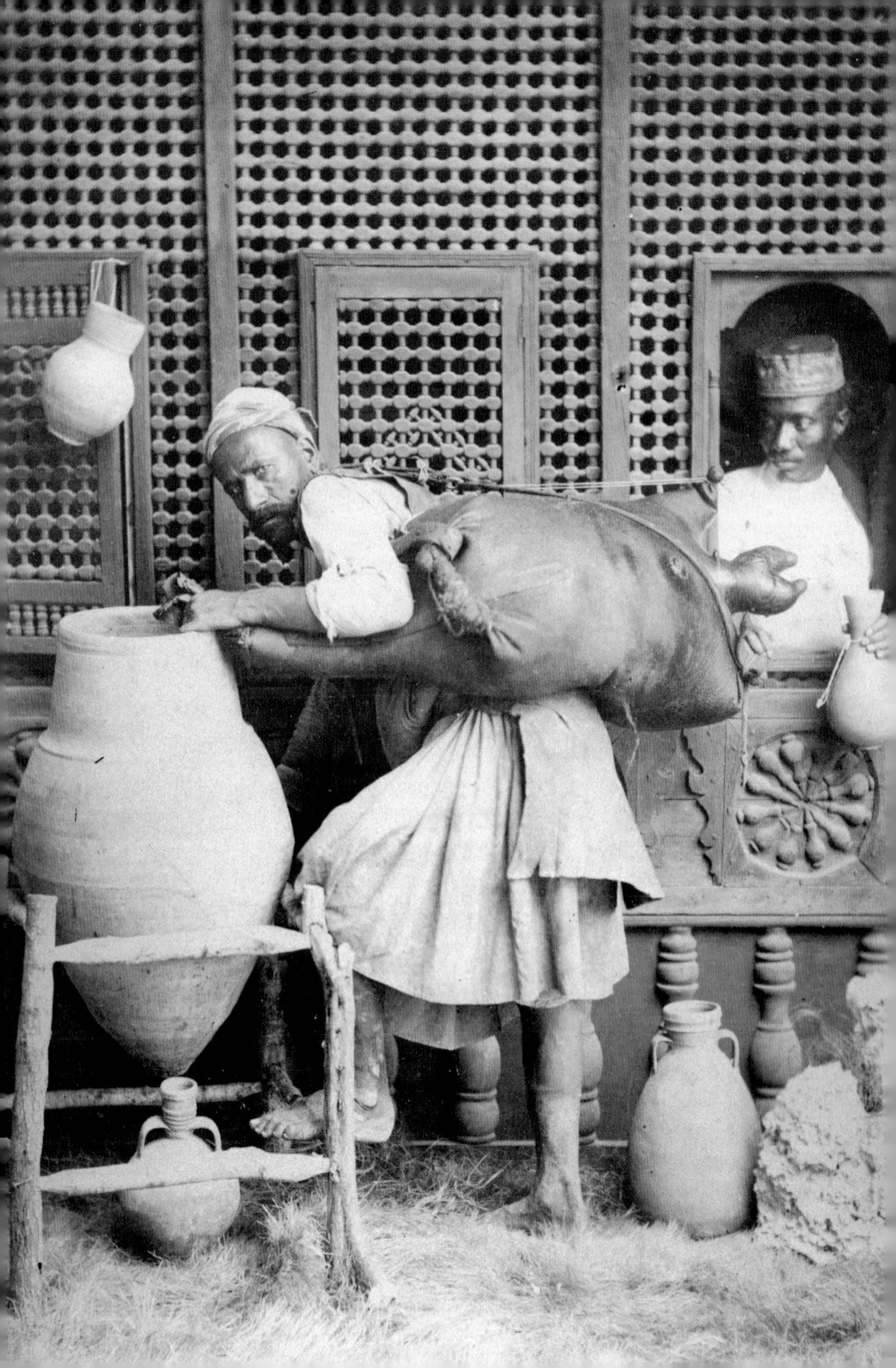

TAKING THE GRAND TOUR OF EGYPT

Barber's shop, c. 1880, photographer unknown, from an album of the Grand Tour assembled in 1890 by a tourist identified only as 'H. M.'.

At Giza, by the mid 1860s, there were already several souvenir stalls selling photographs in a variety of sizes. By the end of the following decade, their number had swollen considerably. Among the photographers, Antonio Beato, the Zangaki brothers and Hippolyte Arnoux figured strongly.

Perhaps surprisingly, many of the photographs are anonymous save for a serial number, the significance of which has been long since lost. Among those images are many staged groups and tableaux intended to show how 'real' Egyptians led their lives. From the earliest days of Nile package tours, the average tourist would only rarely have encountered local people on their travels.

Large prints – measuring 11 by 9 inches – were typical of the output of most of the Nile photographers. With a wealthy clientele, there was little demand for smaller formats. Bringing back large photographs was a very obvious statement of affluence.

Opposite: Egyptian water carriers, photographer unknown, also from H. M.'s album.

111

Local women were popular subjects for the photographers of the period, and willingly posed for photographs in return for a small fee. One tourist on the Nile wrote in 1889:

The women with their water pots hold the neck of the vessel to the stream till it is filled, and with wonderful celerity elevate the heavy pitcher to the top of the head and balance themselves, often up very steep banks, with apparent ease and speed.

Other popular photographs included the various 'rites of passage' undertaken during the journeys along the Nile. 'We drove to the Pyramids of Gizeh yesterday,' wrote Mary Garnett on 27 February 1894, 'and Lily and Mr H. M. were lugged up. Had about four arabs each.'

The Sphinx, c. 1885 by the Zangaki brothers.

The Garnetts' chosen view of the ascent was the Zangaki brothers' eloquent summary of the relationship between the English tourists and the Egyptians. The formality of the tourists at ground level is gradually replaced as they ascend, their dependence on the dragomans increasing as they climb. For Victorian women, such familiarity was a new and not always welcome experience. Some men revelled in the amusement of the spectacle.

Mark Twain summed it up beautifully in 1868 in *The Innocents Abroad*: 'Who shall say it is not a lively, exhilarating, lacerating, muscle-straining, bone-wrenching and perfectly excruciating pastime, climbing the Pyramids?'

Others saw it differently. In 1874 Eliza Ferguson's husband James wrote in despair to her mother, so affronted was he by what he saw as the unwarranted intimacy which his wife's ascent of the pyramids seemed to require:

When on the 10th of February last she solemnly promised to be a faithful and loving wife, I thought, as most of us probably did, that she would; but, alas! what a terrible revulsion my feelings have undergone! If I were to tell you how many strange men she hugged last Monday, not to mention those into whose arms she jumped, and allowing herself to be supported and carried, you would hold up your hands in horror. I daresay she may explain this away in some crooked style of her own, probably by telling you that the attention of the former was necessary to support her on a donkey which she was riding, and those which she had on Monday were necessary for her safety in the ascent of the Pyramids; but these miserable subterfuges we can easily see through.

No further mention of the matter was ever made – and the marriage survived.

The process of being pushed and hauled up the huge stone blocks had, apparently, not changed by 1905, when Max Rudmann's postcard view (overleaf) was published.

Above: A posed studio group, 'Egyptian Women', one of many images showing Egyptian dress and culture; photographer unknown, c. 1880.

Egyptian women carrying water; photographer unknown, c. 1880.

THE VICTORIAN AND EDWARDIAN TOURIST

From H. M.'s 1890 album, this study is titled 'Nubians' and was taken c. 1885 by Hippolyte Arnoux, a French photographer based in Port Said. Arnoux was best known for his studies of the Suez Canal, and, in addition to his studio in the Place des Consules, he had a darkroom boat on the canal itself.

Victualling a steamer off Port Said, c. 1906. Local men carried both food and coal aboard in baskets.

114

TAKING THE GRAND TOUR OF EGYPT

A tourist ascending the Great Pyramid, Cairo; a postcard of c. 1905, published by Cairo-based Max H. Rudmann. Rudmann published a large range of postcards for both the French and British tourist markets, helpfully issuing them with captions in either French or English.

Camels before the Great Pyramid, Giza, 1906. By the Edwardian years, the picture postcard had taken on the role of the large photographic print. The cost of undertaking the Egyptian tour had reduced significantly over the preceding decade, opening the experience up to the middle classes. 'Our party ascended this,' wrote Ada to her friend in Birmingham in April 1908. ' The heat is tremendous. We are both well and full of wonderment.'

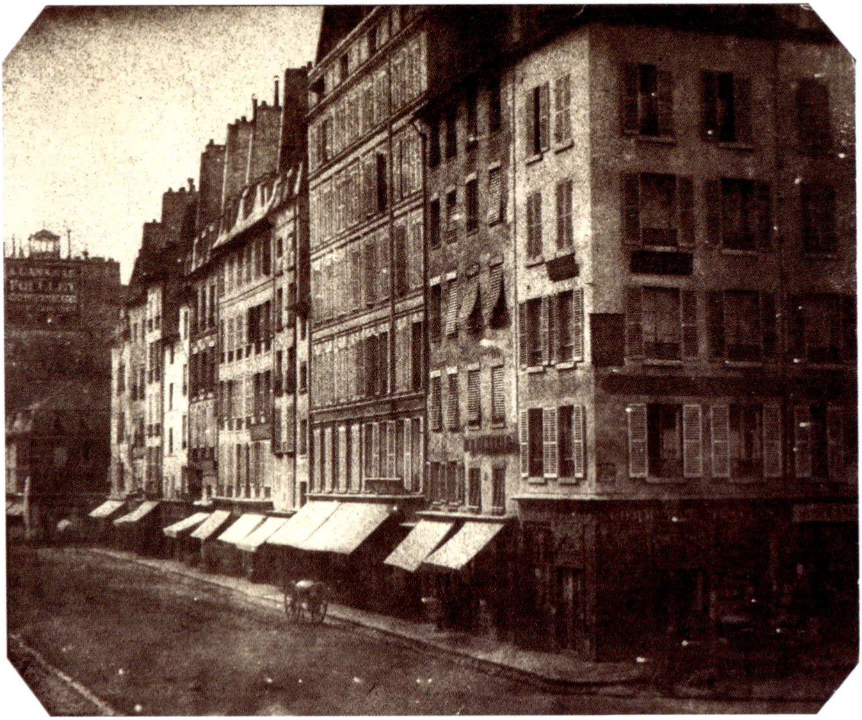

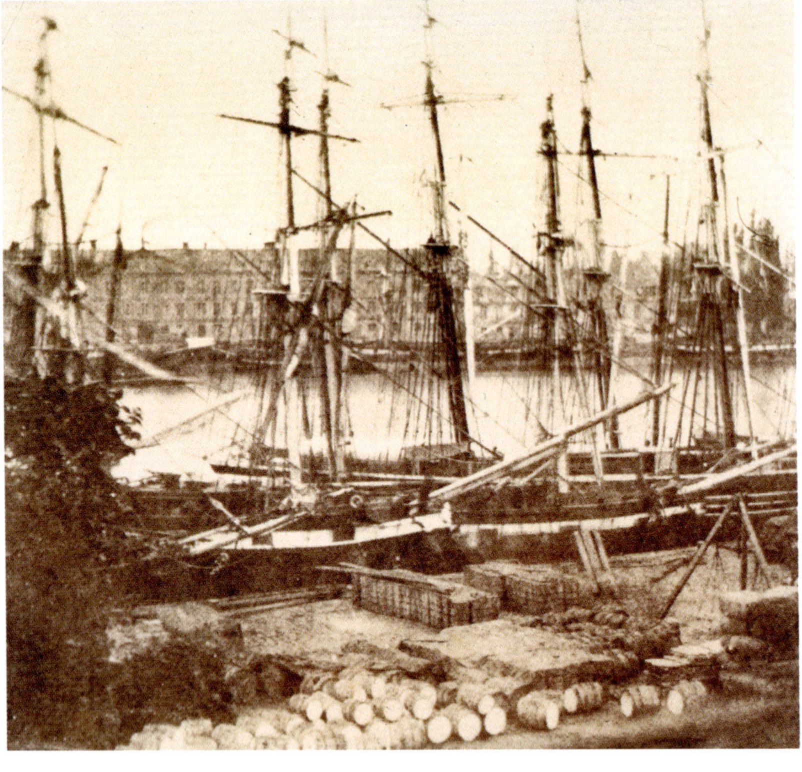

TOURING WITH A CAMERA

WHEN THE FIRST practicable photographic process was invented in the 1840s, it required large and bulky cameras, a great deal of time, and a lot of skill – and the photographer had to transport all the paraphernalia usually found in the studio and the darkroom to the chosen location.

William Henry Fox Talbot has often been described as the father of modern photography. At his home in Lacock, Wiltshire, he invented the idea of the negative from which countless prints could be made, and he also produced the first photographically illustrated books, as well as pioneering many of the uses to which we put photography today. He was a wealthy man, able to afford to travel throughout Britain and into Europe, so it is hardly surprising that he created some of what may be described as the prototypes of the tourist images we still produce today.

Talbot and his assistant Nicholaas Henneman travelled to France in May 1843, arriving in Calais on the 12th, and made their way to Paris and Rouen, making calotype views along the way. Talbot was combining a business trip – intended to popularise his calotype paper negative process – with a chance to photograph some of France's great cathedrals. Even though photography was in its infancy, he was thwarted at Rouen, where he was told that someone already had exclusive rights to photograph the cathedral.

So it is not just today that tourist photographers come up against 'no photography' rules. When Talbot arrived in Rouen intent on photographing the cathedral, practical photography was less than five years old, and already there were exclusive franchise arrangements in place. So he photographed the harbour instead, producing some of the earliest surviving photographs of ships.

From the many calotypes he made during his two months travelling in France, a Paris street scene (a view taken from the window of his room at the Hôtel de Douvres) and a view of the cathedral at Orléans would be published in the following year as plates II and XII in his pioneering partwork *The Pencil of Nature*, the world's first photographically illustrated partwork, and the world's first photographically illustrated book.

It was hardly surprising that the majority of early amateur photographers were wealthy people who had a considerable amount of free time. Cameras were expensive hand-built instruments, the processes were slow, exposure times long, and good results not always assured. Taking a photograph was a lengthy and time-consuming undertaking. Early professional photographers

Opposite top: A street in Paris, May 1843, from a calotype paper negative by William Henry Fox Talbot. Long exposures meant that people on the street were reduced to ghostly blurs.

Opposite bottom: Talbot's view of the harbour at Rouen, 16 May 1843. To avoid any movement during the long exposure times then necessary, ships were usually photographed beached at low tide.

THE VICTORIAN AND EDWARDIAN TOURIST

Right: Designed for the travelling photographer, this backpack contained camera, tripod, plates, chemicals and portable darkroom tent.

Below: A photographer and assistant at work, 1860s.

could at least look to earn a profit from their exertions, but for the amateur the pleasure was simply that of successfully negotiating the intricacies of the procedure.

Help for the travelling photographer came as early as 1857, when *The Photographic Tourist* by Frederick J. Cox was published – the first book aimed specifically at those wishing to take a camera with them on their excursions. A second edition followed in 1858, with a third in 1861, so clearly the idea was a popular one.

For the photographers' families, the idea may have been less popular: taking a camera on a touring holiday, whether at home or abroad, involved transporting several trunks full of chemicals, dishes, sheets of glass, and usually a portable darktent in which to develop the negatives, all in addition to their own luggage.

The Reverend Thomas Melville Raven, whose photographic tour of France has

Dryburgh Abbey, 1857, attributed to Dr Thomas Keith, an eminent surgeon who worked with Sir James Young Simpson and Joseph Lister. Keith, a keen amateur photographer, used the waxed paper process, which enabled him to develop his large paper negatives when he got back to his overnight accommodation.

118

A wet plate photographer's camera and darktent.

already been mentioned, was one such early photographic tourist, so his wife and friends were destined to spend a large proportion of their trip waiting while he set up his cumbersome camera and mobile darkroom – and waiting for the right weather conditions. With long exposures, even a light wind would reduce trees to mere blurs, and, perhaps surprisingly, early processes worked better in soft light – cloudy conditions – rather than bright sunlight. In sunshine dark shadows became solid, black and impenetrable.

Raven experienced his first encounter with French customs officials when trying to take all his chemicals into the country. After spending hours waiting while the contents of every bottle in his portmanteau were checked against an official list, he recounted that:

> It was beginning to get dark, and I was the last in the room; the case in which my iodized papers were kept had still to be examined, but they were sick of photography and allowed it to pass unopened, much to my satisfaction.

His wife was probably also already sick of photography by the time he was allowed to proceed – and the holiday had not yet even started.

This was an age of innovation: the new medium of photography was improving rapidly, and cameras quickly evolved from the 'sliding box' design, where focus was achieved by sliding one wooden box inside another, to lighter, folding bellows cameras of the style which would dominate the market for photography's first eighty years. One of the first of these, the Kinnear camera, was designed by the Scottish amateur photographer Charles Kinnear especially for his 1857 tour of France. Reducing the weight he had to carry was a

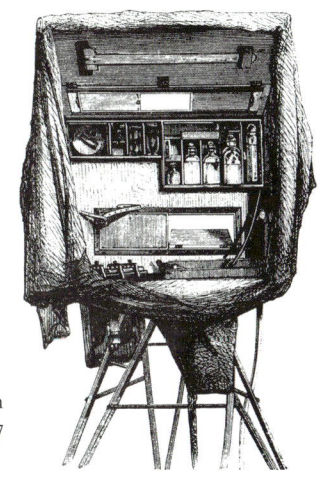

An Ottewill folding camera from the 1860s, based on Kinnear's 1857 design.

A typical portable darktent from the late 1850s and 1860s.

J. Traill Taylor, former editor of *The British Journal of Photography*, said of this view of the south choir aisle of Tintern Abbey, photographed by Horatio Nelson King, that it was 'replete with all those elements which conduce to attract', and concluded that it was 'a pile which, in respect of romantic and picturesque associations, as well as elegance of structure, has few compeers'.

primary concern. Cameras were still huge – his took photographs measuring 11 by 9 inches, on large sheets of sensitised waxed paper, but this was a much less cumbersome option than large glass plates, especially when he and his fellow photographic tourists were journeying from Edinburgh to Normandy.

It was not until the late 1860s that aspiring photographers could buy a box of plates ready to use – until then, they had to coat their own – but the arrival of the 'dry plate' significantly increased the numbers interested in photography as a hobby.

Early photographic magazines and instruction manuals exhorted the amateur to consider the beauty of what they were photographing, and to take the pleasures of their hobby beyond the simple satisfaction of getting an image – any image – at the end of their endeavours.

They were urged to consider photography as an art as well as a science, to compose their images with care and sympathy to their subjects, and to consider everything from the weather to the nature and quality of the light, before taking the lens cap off their cameras. For their families, all those additional considerations probably only slowed proceedings even further.

So just what were photographers seeking to do when they visited and photographed the romantic ruins of medieval abbeys, priories and castles?

TOURING WITH A CAMERA

Three snapshots from a tourist album compiled during a visit to South Africa in 1899. Early tourist albums were already starting to show the same curiosity which marks tourist images today – recording scenes which the visitor had never before experienced: oxen pulling heavily laden passenger coaches across the veldt, and oxen being harnessed up to pull freight wagons, as well as the expected snapshots of the hotels the tourists stayed in. These photographs were probably taken using a 5x4 inch film-pack camera – so neither lightweight nor quick and easy to use.

THE VICTORIAN AND EDWARDIAN TOURIST

Four snapshots from an album compiled during a package tour of the Netherlands in 1901. As cameras became more portable, it became easier to capture the everyday things which make foreign travel different – so dog carts, street vendors and a harbour were popular subjects. One of the author's great aunts is in the group photograph.

An answer to that question can be found in an article published in the *Liverpool & Manchester Photographic Journal* by the Manchester photographer James Mudd. In his essay 'The Artistic Arrangement of the Photographic Landscape', Mudd observed:

> What delightful hours have we passed in wandering through the quiet ruins of some venerable abbey, impressing with wondrous truth, upon the delicate tablets we carried, the marvellous beauty of Gothic window, of broken column, and ivy wreathed arch. How pleasant our visits to moss green old churches, and stately castles, and a thousand pretty nooks, in the shady wood by the river side or in the hedge rows, where the twining wild convolvulus, the bramble, the luxuriant fern, have arrested us…

In other words, the Victorian romantic ideal was nature slowly reasserting itself over the puny efforts of men, the artistry of the medieval mason and sculptor being slowly softened and eroded by time and by nature. And it was the photographer's duty to immortalise that.

Personalising these photographs was far from the minds of the early photographic tourists. Photography was seen as a formal activity, far removed from the casual moments we record today.

Life was becoming easier for the travelling amateur when H. Baden Pritchard wrote his *Continental Rambles with a Camera* in 1883, advising: 'With dry plates, a light half-plate camera, and two or three in the party, there is no reason why the photographic apparatus should not be carried personally in addition to a light knapsack.'

He added a cautionary note on the time necessary for photography in those days:

> Six plates in a tourist journey is ample for a day's work, and sometimes four will suffice very well, for it will be found, practically, that half-an-hour is taken up on average at each exposure, as you have, moreover, your distance to walk in the day, two or three hours is the utmost you can devote to photography.

As cameras became smaller and lighter, plates became more sensitive to light, and exposure times became shorter, the number of tourists with cameras increased dramatically, but until the closing decades of the nineteenth century it remained a hobby which demanded much of its participants.

The Coronation Sports and Games, Pitlochry, 1902: a snapshot taken with a Kodak folding camera.

Ross's 1905 new model twin-lens reflex camera was advertised as being light enough to be used by ladies.

Below: Eastman was aware that some of those who bought his new Kodak 'detective' camera might even wish to develop their own photographs, rather than send the camera back to the factory. He published simple step-by-step instruction leaflets to assist them.

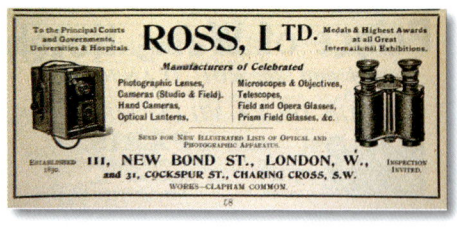

Everything changed when George Eastman created the simple box camera which, loaded with its long roll of negative material, made photography a casual undertaking rather than a formal one. During its development, he called his new device his 'little breast camera', but by January 1888 he had christened it the 'Kodak', a name chosen because it was unlike any other word, entirely memorable, and equally suitable for every language.

Eastman's vision was groundbreaking, and he described his idea eloquently in *The Kodak Primer*:

Will any sane man or woman (for there are thousands of lady votaries of the photographic art) maintain that the necessity of going through ten specific operations, the omission of any one of which would irrevocably spoil the work, does not detract from what would otherwise be a delightful pastime?

But he did much more than just invent a new camera format and type: Eastman took the messy side of photography out of the hands of the photographer, literally, and placed it in the hands of skilled technicians. Many of those who had revelled in their ability to manage every stage of the chemistry thought this was a retrograde step, but, for the majority, photography suddenly became a practical possibility. Gone was the need to carry a large bulky camera, tripod, glass plates and dark slides. In its place came a lightweight camera which could be carried easily in a shoulder bag.

Eastman wrote that 'The principle of the Kodak system is the separation of the work that any person whomsoever can do in making a photograph, from the work only an expert can do', and that his camera could 'be employed without preliminary study, without a dark room, and without chemicals'.

For the first time, people could take photographs without needing to worry about the science of the process. This freedom did not come cheaply, though. The camera cost 5 guineas in Britain, $25 in the United States, and came ready to take one hundred pictures on a paper-based stripping film. Initially, therefore, it was by no means an inexpensive way of taking up photography.

Once the hundred exposures had been made, the camera was parcelled up and returned to the factory, where the pictures were developed, and the camera was reloaded with a new roll of negative material – the total processing and reloading cost being 2 guineas.

The original camera used a paper negative, but in 1889 Eastman moved to the transparent film with which photographers would remain familiar for more than a century, until digital consigned it to history.

The slogan 'You press the button, we do the rest' was genuinely what the Eastman Company offered its customers. Over the next two decades, travelling with a camera was transformed, and the era of the holiday snap was born.

Within only two years, Eastman's range of cameras had been expanded considerably and the simplified Kodak approach to photography had been extended to embrace most of the negative sizes with which photographers were already quite familiar.

Below left:
A very early developing and printing wallet, c. 1900, from Kodak. The camera held by the 'Kodak girl' in the central oval is the folding pocket Kodak camera of 1897.

Left: Eastman introduced his first Kodak camera in 1888. It brought undreamed-of simplicity to the hobby of photography. A simple piece of string cocked the shutter, a button on the side exposed the picture, and a key mechanism advanced the hundred-frame paper negative roll.

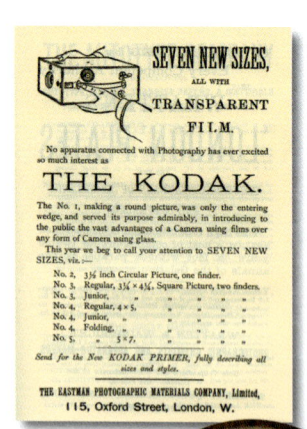

As demand grew, prices fell, with box cameras from rival makers soon available for a few shillings, but, as Kodak's advertising warned, 'If it isn't an Eastman, it isn't a Kodak'. Despite that caution, 'kodaking' quickly became a commonly used term for the taking of snapshots.

As the snapshot craze gained popularity, the traditional family album holding carte-de-visite prints taken by professionals was replaced by albums specially designed to take a variety of different sizes of Kodak snapshots.

With lighter and easier-to-use cameras, the Edwardian era brought a dramatic increase in the popularity of tourist photography. While, for many, buying postcards of the places they visited remained sufficient, for others only their own personal photographic memories told the real story. The Kodak camera gave everyone control of his or her visual memories, and initiated the democratisation of photography, where the snapshotter's own ideas of what were the key visual reminders of his or her travel experience assumed significance. The personal relevance of the images quickly became more important than their technical and visual qualities.

But not everyone approved. The great American photographer Alfred Stieglitz, writing in 1897, dismissed the hand camera as 'the beginning of the photography-by-the-yard era' in which 'ranks of enthusiastic Button-Pressers were enlarged to enormous dimensions'. He went on:

The small instrument [was] innocent enough in itself, but terrible in the hands of the unknowing, as a mere toy, good for the purposes of the globe-trotter, who wished to jot down photographic notes as he passed along his journey, but in no way adapted to him whose aim is to do serious work.

He also believed that the craze for snapshot photography would quickly give way to the growing enthusiasm for cycling. Time would, very quickly, prove him wrong.

Film outlets became established at key scenic locations on world tourist trails, just as prints by the leading photographers had done half a century earlier. Print sales kiosks at places such as the pyramids continued to sell large-format photographs for some years, but they did so alongside postcards and rolls of film.

TOURING WITH A CAMERA

Before 1910, there was even the opportunity to photograph in real colour, albeit on glass plates once again. The French Autochrome process, first marketed in 1907, was, however, for the more serious traveller with a camera. A complex process using grains of potato starch dyed red, green and blue could, in the hands of an accomplished user, produce some wonderfully realistic colour slides on glass plates which, when held up to the light, reproduced all the brilliance of colour in the original subjects. The plates were slow, so exposure times were long – returning photography to the exposures of five to ten seconds which had been commonplace half a century earlier.

While the majority of holidaymakers with cameras simply photographed the places they visited and the people they travelled with – much as today – for others the photographs they brought back were just the starting point for a lot of darkroom work over the winter months, to create unique artistic images. While adopting roll film, they eschewed the simplest cameras for instruments with high-quality lenses, allowing them to retain control over exposure, focus, etc.

Whatever their motivation, for a significant majority of tourists, travelling with a camera had, by the end of the Edwardian era, become the norm.

Autochromes taken in 1910 by amateur photographer W. Wilson in the conservatories at Stamford Park, Lancashire. His exposures, twenty and thirty-five seconds. were noted on the edges of the plates.

Bank manager Alexander Wilson Hill's 1910 'bromoil' study of the fishwives of Tarbert on the west coast of Scotland.

INDEX

Page numbers in italics refer to illustrations

Abraham Brothers Keswick, 70,
Allinari, Fratelli *98*, 99
Arnoux, Hippolyte 111, *114*
Autochrome *127*
Baedeker, Karl 51, 68
Baedeker's guides 48–51, 75, 101
Bassett-Lowke, W. J. 72
Beato, Antonio *107–8*, 111
Bedford, Francis 28
Bierstadt, Charles 48
Black, Adam & Charles 39, 47, 69, 72
Bradford Exhibition 1904, 8
Bradshaw, George 46
Braun, Adolphe 48, 99
Brillié-Schneider *85*
Burns, George and James 53–4
Caitlin's Royal Pierrots 14
Caledonian MacBrayne 53
Caledonian Railway 54
Caledonian Steam Packet Company 54
Continental Rambles with a Camera 123
Cook, Ernest 37
Cook, John Mason 26, 35,
Cook, Thomas Jnr 37
Cook, Thomas 13, 15–16, 18, 24–37, 51, 70–72, 80–82, *83*, 85, *104*, *106–7*
Coupil et Cie, Paris 99
Cox & Kings 10
Cox, Frederick J. 118
Cunard, Samuel 54
Defoe, Daniel 38, 41

Dropping Stone, Gilsland 8
Eastman, George 123–6
Exposition Universelle, Paris 1855, 80–81
Fenton, Roger 9
Ferguson, James and Eliza 25, 83, 85, 112–13
Focus magazine 77–8
Frith, Francis 17, 70
Furness Railway Company 71
Garnett, Mary and Robert 85–6, 103, 106, 108, 112
Grand Tour 7
Grasmere Sports 71
Great Eastern Railway 42
Great Exhibition, 1851 32–4
Henneman, Nicholaas 117
Hill, Alexander Wilson *127*
Hill, Olivia 65
Hutcheson, David & Company 53–4, 58
Japanese-British Exhibition 11
Johnstone, John 43, 45
Jones, Reverend Calvert Richard 92, *94–5*
Keith, Dr. Thomas *118*
Keswick Convention 72–3
King, Horatio Nelson *120*
Kinnear, Charles 79, 119
Kodak 123–6
Lakeside & Haverthwaite Railway 71
Lancaster & Carlisle Railway Company 41

Liverpool & Manchester Photographic Journal 122
London Stereoscopic & Photographic Company 9
London, Victoria Station 7
London, White City 11
MacBrayne, David 53–63
Manchester Photographic Company 68
Midland Railway 27
Miss Costello's North Wales 45
Mudd, James 122
Muirhead, James and Findlay 49, 75
Naya, Carlo *88*, 89
North Western Railway 41
Ogle, Thomas 69
Pappayanni Line 85
Pennant, Thomas 40–41
Pescio & de Carré 99
Pettit, Alfred 70
Philipse & Lees, photographers 20
Photochrom Company of Zurich 19, 21, 26, 74, *100*
Photographic Notes 79
Ponti, Carlo *88–9*, 89, 92
Potter, Beatrix 65
Pritchard, H. Baden 123
Raven, Reverend Thomas Melville 77–9, 118–19
Ravenglass & Eskdale Railway 72
Rawnsley, Canon Hardwicke 65
Ritchie, Leitch 83
Roger, Charles, 1851 *A*

Week in Bridge of Allan by 9–10
Ross Ltd *124*
Rudman, Max 113, *115*
Ruskin, John 65
Scott, Sir Walter 12–13, 43–4
Smith, W.H. & Sons 43, 46
Sommer, Giorgio 97, 99
South Eastern Railway *84*, 85
Steiglitz, Alfred 126
'Sylvan' Handbooks 38, 42–4, 65–7, 69–71
Talbot, Kit 92
Talbot, William Henry Fox 10, 12–13, 92, 94, *116*, 117
Taylor, J. Traill 120
Thomson, John 48
Thomson, Stephen 48
Treasure Spots of the World 47–9
Turner, J.M.W. 81, 82–3
Twain, Mark 101–3, 112
Valentine, James 17, 30–31, 39, 44, *68*
Victoria, Queen 7, 12, 43, 56, 58, 60
Walmesley Brothers 74, 75
Ward, Locke & Tyler 47
Wilson, George Washington 17, 26, 64, 70
Windermere Cruises 71
Woodbury, Walter Bentley 47–9
Wordsworth, William 65
Zangaki Brothers *104*, 105, *107*, 109, 111, 112

128